Praise for

PEACE ECONOMICS

"The effect of violence on economic progress is very strong, yet it has not received appropriate attention. Jurgen Brauer and J. Paul Dunne have performed a great service by combining general economic perspectives with case studies to survey economic growth in its broadest aspects, in particular stressing the role of internal and external conflict."
—**Kenneth J. Arrow,** Nobel Laureate and Joan Kenney Professor of Economics and professor of operations research, Stanford University

"*Peace Economics* is essential reading for any person interested in understanding and assessing the costs of war and how to create real incentives to secure a stable peace. It illuminates the political economy of war and peace brilliantly. The twelve design principles for building peaceful institutions and the four policy lessons brilliantly provide policymakers and concerned citizens with economic and social tools to rebuild trust, social capital, and cooperative harmonious social and political relationships. I heartily commend this book to anyone interested in ensuring that the twenty-first century is an age of maturity and peacefulness."
—**Kevin P. Clements,** foundation chair and director, National Centre for Peace and Conflict Studies, University of Otago, Dunedin, New Zealand, and past secretary general, International Peace Research Association

"The volume entitled *Peace Economics: A Macroeconomic Primer for Violence-Afflicted States* will be the bible for all peace economists. Jurgen Brauer and J. Paul Dunne, two of the most distinguished peace economists, have produced a timely, nuanced, and excellent book that painstakingly collects the artifacts of modern macroeconomics with relevant social and cultural ammunitions needed for developing the analytical foundation of peace economics. This volume will be an important and decisive step toward dismantling the sophistry of peace economics built solely on economic principles."

—**Partha Gangopadhyay,** editor-in-chief, *International Journal of Development and Conflict,* and associate professor, School of Economics and Finance, University of Western Sydney

"Most economics is peace economics in that it assumes away violence, but violence is endemic and economic processes do influence the incentive to use violence. This book takes the violence seriously and examines how macroeconomic policy can contribute to keeping or restoring the peace. It presents the basic economic principles in a way that is relevant to practitioners facing the challenge of reducing violence or trying to promote post-conflict reconstruction. The key policy lessons and tips are summarized at each stage and the final chapter looks at how to design and promote peace. Brauer and Dunne very effectively condense a large amount of technical material into a form that policymakers in states afflicted by violence will find very useful."

—**Ron Smith,** professor of applied economics, Birkbeck College, University of London

"Why should economists care about conflict and violence? Brauer and Dunne have a very convincing answer: Not only has conflict economic costs and causes that hinder long-run development, but conflict is also part of the very nature of economics. Predation and plunder, as well as production and exchange, are means of resource allocation. This book is a mandatory reference for academics and practitioners interested in the macroeconomics of conflict-affected states, and in how to make peace enduring and resilient."

—**Juan Vargas,** professor of economics, Universidad del Rosario

PEACE ECONOMICS

UNITED STATES
INSTITUTE OF PEACE
ACADEMY
GUIDES

PEACE ECONOMICS

A MACROECONOMIC PRIMER FOR VIOLENCE-AFFLICTED STATES

JURGEN BRAUER AND J. PAUL DUNNE

UNITED STATES INSTITUTE OF PEACE
Washington, DC

The views expressed in this book are those of the authors alone. They do not necessarily reflect the views of the United States Institute of Peace.

UNITED STATES INSTITUTE OF PEACE
2301 Constitution Avenue, NW
Washington, DC 20037
www.usip.org

First published 2012

To request permission to photocopy or reprint materials for course use, contact the Copyright Clearance Center at www.copyright.com. For print, electronic media, and all other subsidiary rights e-mail permissions@usip.org

Printed in the United States of America

The paper used in this publication meets the minimum requirements of American National Standards for Information Science—Permanence of Paper for Printed Library Materials, ANSI Z39.48-1984.

Library of Congress Cataloging-in-Publication Data

Brauer, Jurgen, 1957-
  Peace economics : a macroeconomic primer for violence-afflicted states / Jurgen Brauer and J. Paul Dunne.
      p. cm. — (United States Institute of Peace Academy guides)
  Includes index.
  ISBN 978-1-60127-138-9 (alk. paper)
  1. Economic stabilization. 2. Economic policy. 3. Macroeconomics. 4. Peace—Economic aspects. 5. War—Economic aspects. I. Dunne, Paul. II. United States Institute of Peace. III. Title.
  HB3732.B73 2012
  339.5—dc23
                    2012017402

Jurgen Brauer dedicates the volume to
my children Jonathan, Leon, and Anne

Paul Dunne dedicates the volume to
my father John

UNITED STATES
INSTITUTE OF PEACE
ACADEMY
GUIDES

Peace Economics is an introduction to the economic factors that surround conflict. These factors may cause conflict or may appear as a result of conflict. Whatever their origin, these factors will complicate efforts to prevent, resolve, or transform conflict so that it can be handled through political means rather than through violence. The objective of this book is to give the nonspecialist an understanding of economics in a conflict situation as well as some suggestions on how to deal with these problems. It grows out of the efforts of USIP's Center for Sustainable Economies, which spearheads the Institute's work on the economic dimensions of conflict management and peace promotion.

The book is the first in the new Academy Guides series. The purpose of the series is to introduce the reader to topics of conflict management and provide explanations of key concepts along with advice on how policymakers and implementers can make use of these concepts as they plan for and initiate operations in conflict zones. Other books in the series will focus on conflict analysis, engaging with identity-based differences, and governance and democratic practices in war-to-peace transitions.

In our rapidly evolving and often unstable global environment, many institutions—including the U.S. government, the United Nations, regional organizations, and dozens of nongovernmental organizations (NGOs)—are devoting resources to preventing conflict and to postconflict operations. However, these organizations vary widely in the training they provide, and many practitioners express a desire for more preparation for these complex operations.

Accordingly, the United States Institute of Peace established the Academy for International Conflict Management and Peacebuilding in 2009 to prepare practitioners to work effectively in conflict zones abroad and to help decision-makers develop effective strategies to prevent and resolve conflicts.

The USIP Academy is a professional education and training center offering practitioner courses on conflict prevention, management, and resolution. Drawing on USIP's twenty-five years of leadership in the field, these courses emphasize strategic thinking and practical skills. They include a mix of theory and practice. Participants come from a wide variety of backgrounds: U.S. government agencies, embassies and foreign ministries of international partners, international organizations, the nonprofit sector, the military, international development agencies, educational institutions, and others. Typically, participants have several years of relevant experience in their fields.

As with the courses, the books should prove especially useful to people from government, the military, NGOs, and civil society who are engaged in conflict management and peacebuilding. They might also find a place in college courses and in bookstores.

We look forward to receiving our readers feedback on this exciting new endeavor. You can reach us at academy@usip.org, and you can check out the latest information on the Institute and the Academy at usip.org.

—*Pamela Aall, Provost*
Academy for International Conflict Management and Peacebuilding
United States Institute of Peace

CONTENTS

ACKNOWLEDGMENTS

This report was commissioned by the Center for Sustainable Economies at the U.S. Institute of Peace (USIP) following a series of meetings on the topic to provide a handbook for scholars and practitioners working on the economics-conflict nexus. The project was managed by Raymond Gilpin, director of USIP's Center for Sustainable Economies in partnership with Economists for Peace and Security (www.epsusa.org). A version of the manuscript was discussed at a review conference held on February 19, 2010, at the offices of USIP in Washington, DC. Recognizing that the following do not represent or speak for the organizations with which they have been or may now be affiliated, we thank for useful comments Jomana Amara, Matt Barger, Colleen Callahan, Raymond Gilpin, Corine Graff, Nate Hagen, Thea Harvey, Michael Hazilla, Peter Howells, Willene Johnson, Amanda Mayoral, Berhanu Mengistu, Norm Olsen, Basel Saleh, and Ron Smith. We are grateful to Brian Slattery and the USIP Press staff for editing and producing this Guide. The views expressed in this text are solely the authors' and do not necessarily reflect those of the Institute or its staff.

SUMMARY

- Creating sound economic policy and a stable macroeconomic frame-work have become central concepts in peace negotiations and state-building efforts, yet few practitioners have the economic background needed to apply these concepts effectively in their work. This publica-tion, a primer on macroeconomic fundamentals as they touch on vio-lence-afflicted states, seeks to address this problem.

- The primer covers economic development, economic growth, macro-economic stabilization, and global trade and finance in both theory and practice, with a particular focus on the ways in which violence and the recovery from violence affect them all. Though the economic effects of violence are difficult to quantify for a variety of reasons, it is clear that war and other violent conflict have almost entirely negative economic effects, both during active fighting and long thereafter. Carefully crafted peace agreements, well-designed economic policy, and effective aid, however, can alleviate the economic damage done and thus reduce the chance of a relapse into violence.

- Designing peace from an economic perspective—and creating the in-stitutions that can implement the policies stemming from peace agreements—ultimately calls for practitioners to adhere to principles that aim to redraw the social contract and reestablish social capital, both among leaders and between the eventual governments and the public. The principles cannot guarantee success, but as both theory and the legacy of negotiated peace treaties since the end of the Cold War have shown, they can improve the chances of creating a stronger peace.

INTRODUCTION

> The economic problem of reconstruction is that of rebuilding the capital of
> society.... Reconstruction is merely a special case of economic progress. If we
> are to understand its problems thoroughly, we must examine what is meant
> by economic progress and try to discover how it comes about.[1]
> —Kenneth E. Boulding

Without economics there can be neither war nor peace. Economic grievances—such as severely uneven distributions of wealth, lack of income-
earning opportunities, or disputes over natural resources—can give rise to
war. During war, economic forces both provide and destroy resources. And
after war, well-functioning production and exchange mechanisms need to
be put back together again, or else relapse into war is likely.

As aggressors or victims, even robustly performing economies can fall
prey to armed violence and its devastating economic consequences. The
cases of Japan, Germany, and the eventually victorious powers in World
War II (1939–45) attest to this. Economic aspects related to labor, capital,
trade, and finance can motivate, drive, prolong, and terminate violence, as
seen in the civil wars of both the United States (1861–65) and Mozambique
(1976–92). To prosecute war, warriors need to volunteer, be hired, or be

conscripted, and bullets need to be manufactured, bought, and sold. When the guns fall silent, postwar economics determines the prospects for peace, as communities and livelihoods need to be rebuilt. While the economic terms and execution of the post–World War I peace treaty helped lay the foundations for World War II, the post–World War II peace arrangements helped create the economic miracles of both Germany and Japan. The same logic applies, we now know, to armed violence in much of the developing world in Africa, Asia, and Latin America. The proper design and implementation of economic policies and their supporting institutions can be among the primary instruments for preventing armed violence—including criminal violence that may follow a peacemaking accord in a state with a broken social contract.

This volume is a primer on macroeconomic fundamentals as they touch on violence-afflicted states, focusing on emerging and developing economies even as it includes lessons learned from advanced economies. Economists, of course, are hard put to define fundamentals, let alone agree on just what they are, and the finance-driven world economic crisis of the late 2000s has illustrated that economic theories, policies, and regulations are less firmly set in place than it was once thought they were. In this regard, we use the word *primer* to mean a general-purpose overview of important economic principles to keep in mind, not a specific how-to guide—akin to a manual on how to understand the mechanics and operation of combustion engines generally, rather than on how to fix a specific engine. Engines and economies alike can sputter and break in many ways, but when restored, they all need to perform the same general functions, in a certain sequence, and such that their various elements are balanced against each other.

In the economics of peace, there is the danger of missing the forest for the trees. Practitioners tend to focus on the trees: They are keen to answer the question of what to do when specific problems arise in the field. The answer partly depends, however, on what the desired healthy forest is to look like. The economics of peace can be understood as an ecosystem, and fixing one's gaze on design principles rather than on context specifics assists not only postwar reconstruction but also violence prevention, mitigation, and building immunity and resilience to violence. Thus, the purpose of the primer extends beyond pure economics into the wider realm of social reconstitution, contract, and capital, in the hopes of helping practitioners build a stronger and more stable peace. One might think of this as peace engineering.

The primer's five chapters explain key concepts and relationships in layperson's terms; present important topics, issues, data, and metrics; outline the roles and responsibilities of key institutions; and offer lessons for violence prevention, mediation, peace agreements, and postviolence management. They conclude with illustrative cases to highlight missteps as well as good practice. This primer is no substitute for an economics textbook, but the theory, lessons, and cases it contains should assist practitioners in employing economics to create more stable peace.

Chapter 1 provides information on violence and economic performance, discusses the purpose of economics and the many facets of economic policy and politics, and looks at some of the links between violence and economic development. Chapter 2 provides an overview of economic growth theory and policy. Policymakers sometimes fail to appreciate that growth is a means to an end—the betterment of life—and not an end in itself.[2] The chapter discusses how economic performance is measured, as well as the purposes and policies of some important economic institutions. Chapter 3 moves from long-term to short-term considerations, or, in the jargon of the profession, to macroeconomic stabilization theory and policy. In practice this means fiscal and monetary policy, concerned with taxation, the setting of interest rates, and the spillover effects of these on other policy and development goals. Chapter 4 turns from closed to open economics, that is, to international trade and finance theory and policy. Chapter 5 concludes by offering rules of thumb that peace negotiators and economic policymakers may find useful. It ties the preceding chapters together and discusses them in regard to issues pertaining to the design of peace. These include considerations of social contract.

Already, however, four lessons emerge. Without economics there is neither war nor peace. The design and execution of postwar economic policy help determine the success or failure of efforts to create peace. The proper design and implementation of economic policy can be among the primary instruments for preventing violence in the first place. Finally, focusing on the basic mechanics of economic engines in general rather than on fixing specific broken engines—that is, focusing on purpose and design—can assist with postviolence reconstruction and building long-term immunity and resilience to violence.

Notes

1. Kenneth E. Boulding, *The Economics of Peace* (New York: Prentice-Hall, 1945), 4, 73.

2. J.E. Stiglitz, A. Sen, and J.-P. Fitoussi, *Report by the Commission on the Measurement of Economic Performance and Social Progress* (Paris: Commission on the Measurement of Economic Performance and Social Progress, 2009), available at www.stiglitz-sen-fitoussi.fr (accessed December 6, 2011).

1

VIOLENCE AND
ECONOMIC DEVELOPMENT

The Economic Cost of Violence: A First Impression

The World Health Organization (WHO) differentiates among forms of violence by grouping them into three categories: self-harm (including suicide), interpersonal violence (e.g., violence between intimate partners and other forms of family violence; rape and sexual assault by strangers; violence committed in institutional settings, such as schools, prisons, and workplaces), and collective violence (e.g., armed conflict between, among, and within states; violent political repression and genocide; violent acts of terror; organized crime). Together, these form an ecology of violence progressing from individual and relationship-related violence to communal and large-scale violence.[1]

According to the World Health Organization, *self-harm* refers to self-directed violence, including suicide. *Interpersonal violence* includes intimate partner and other family violence, assault and homicide, and violence committed in institutional settings. *Collective violence* includes armed conflict between, among, and within states; communal-level violence; violent acts of terror; and organized crime.

Gross domestic product is the monetary value, and hence income, of all goods and services legally produced by residents of a country within one calendar year. *Gross world product* is the sum of gross domestic product across all countries.

The economics of crime is a well-established field of study; more recently, economists and quantitative political scientists have also concentrated on collective forms of violence. In 2008 the United Nations Development Programme (UNDP) Bureau for Crisis Prevention and Recovery examined seven countries, collecting data on their pre- and post-war per capita values of gross domestic product (GDP), adjusting for inflation and purchasing power differences (for an explanation of these terms, see chapter 2 or the glossary). Using revised and updated numbers, figure 1.1 compares the economic record of these seven countries. For ease of comparison, a country's GDP is set equal to an index of 100 for the year in which its war ended, indicated by the vertical dashed line in the figure.[2] An arrow for each state indicates its war's start date. In most cases, before the war began, per capita GDP was growing. With the start of war, or shortly thereafter, GDP collapsed. And with peace, GDP started to grow once more.

Three countries—El Salvador, Guatemala, and Nicaragua—experienced weak postwar growth and hence are designated as weak-growth recovery states. The others—Cambodia, Mozambique, Rwanda, and Uganda—are considered strong-growth recovery states. But the macroeconomic policies of each country differ from the others', as do the trajectories of their recoveries. Rwanda bounced back strongly right after 1994, but over the following ten years experienced two periods of decline. Mozambique floundered in its initial postwar years before starting to grow more strongly. Cambodia's per capita income index plunged to about half its initial value during the war, and only ten years after the war ended recovered to its former income level of thirty years before. Nicaragua's high point in per capita GDP came thirteen years before the end of the war; nineteen years after the end of the war, its income level still was less than one-half of what it once was. In El Salvador average income levels improved slightly postwar, but the peace after the war ended was worse than the war itself. It is said that more people were killed there in the ten years after the war than during the twelve-year conflict.[3]

The UNDP study reports that the economic cost of civil war lies somewhere between 1.7 and 3.3 percent of GDP per country per conflict year before 1990 and averages 12.3 percent of GDP after 1990—that is, in the post–Cold War era.[4] To show the cumulative effects of these losses, figure 1.2 redraws figure 1.1, where the curved, solid black line represents the average

FIGURE 1.1. Inflation-Adjusted Per Capita GDP, Selected Countries Pre- and Postwar

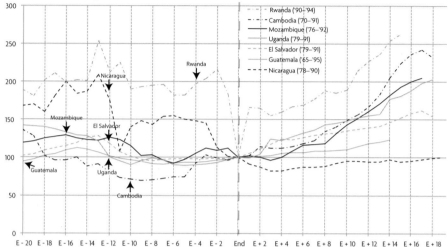

Note: The vertical axis measures inflation-adjusted per capita GDP in purchasing power terms
(base year = 2005). The figure is based on UNDP (2008, p. 111, figure 4.2) but has been updated
by the authors with Penn World Table 7.0 data

Source: Authors' computation from Penn World Table 7.0 data

fall and rise of per capita GDP in the sample during and after war and the dotted line represents the potential GDP growth path had war not interfered. The area in between the lines indicates cumulative GDP losses—which, in the thirty-five years the UNDP study covers, are substantial (see below).

Economists do not agree on how to fully compute or even enumerate the global cost of war, let alone the cost of all violence, war-related or not. What is required is comprehensive and consistent computations of current cost, legacy cost, and spillover cost.[5] The current cost is the direct and indirect cost of violence incurred in a given time period (e.g., a calendar year) and a given geographic space (e.g., within the borders of a country). The legacy cost includes the cost of past violence that carries into the present (e.g., reduced productivity on account of permanent injury; continuous health care for the injured). The spillover cost accounts for costs imposed on bystanders (e.g., refugees from state A that impose a cost on state B). A complete survey of the various estimates found in the literature does not exist, though Brauer and Tepper-Marlin partially survey the economic cost of self-harm, interpersonal, and collective violence, including civil wars and terrorism.[6] They conclude conservatively that, if all violence had ceased, the 2007

FIGURE 1.2. Average and Potential Per Capita GDP Pre- and Postwar

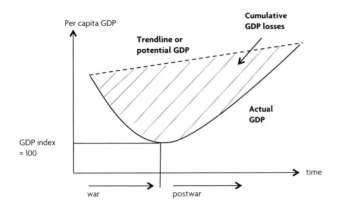

value of world economic production, called gross world product (GWP)—the sum of GDP across all countries—could have been 8.7 percent larger than it actually was. They distinguish between static effects and dynamic effects. The former recognize that cessation of violence makes some security services superfluous, freeing expenditure to be shifted to other goods and services. But this substitution effect does not increase GDP; it merely reallocates spending from one sector of the economy to another. The economic pie does not get larger. However, being more secure about one's person, family, and property liberates energies to undertake productive investment that does increase GDP, and it is this effect of nonviolence that—they suggest—would have amounted to an 8.7 percent gain in GWP in 2007. As an example, a study of Colombia finds that farmers in regions under active civil war threat invested less in irrigation, reducing potential farm output and income derived therefrom.[7]

As violence is a continuous phenomenon, the cost of about 9 percent of GWP represents annually forfeited economic output. In contrast, the International Monetary Fund (IMF) estimates that the world economic crisis of 2009 amounted to a one-time world output loss of a mere 0.5 percent.[8] The world economic crisis would have been worse had it not been for extraordinary policy intervention worldwide. The ongoing, annual violence crisis

The *current cost* of violence is the direct and indirect cost in a given period across a given geographic space. The *legacy cost* is the cost of past violence that carries over to the present. The *spillover cost* is the cost imposed on bystanders.

A *static peace dividend* refers to a redistribution of economic activity from violence-related to nonviolence-related spending. A *dynamic peace dividend* results when security spending can be cut and applied to productivity-enhancing physical, human, institutional, and social capital.

is a much more severe economic problem and demands at least equally extraordinary policy attention and intervention.

Assets, Income, and the Bathtub Theorem

Purpose of Economics

To survive and to reproduce into the next generation, all human and non-human organisms must produce, distribute, and consume. The details vary by species, but the economy of nature is real enough, and biologists routinely apply economic thinking about (energy) costs and (reproductive) benefits to the organisms they study. Whereas other species endlessly struggle for survival, however, the human species is endowed with the seemingly singular capacity to design systems of production, distribution, and consumption that, in principle, permit continual betterment of our condition of life. Among the signal achievements of the human economic system is the pervasive extent of trade. Among nonhumans it tends to be the species that specialize. Among humans it tends to be the individuals within the species that specialize in acquiring a useful skill, the product of which is bartered against the specialized products of other individuals.

The Three Economies

Because of the importance of trade, economists have long focused on the exchange economy. To exchange means to agree on the ratio at which goods and services change hands—whether it is one apple or two apples for an orange, or one or two hours of work for fifteen dollars. The ratio can create conflict because it assigns values to each good or service with consequences that affect distribution and consumption and, hence, material well-being. But as a rule, trading economies are peaceful economies, and vice versa.[9] Inasmuch as war disrupts trade routes and destroys trade facilities, such as roads and ports, restoring and promoting internal and external trade and

> *Economics* deals with the production, distribution, and consumption of the means to livelihood, with the aim of continual betterment of life. Three types of economy are the exchange economy, the grants economy, and the appropriation economy.

the needed infrastructure is therefore important for postwar recovery. We discuss aspects of infrastructure rebuilding later on in this chapter.

A second kind of economy is the grants economy. Grants transfer resources from one potential spender to another, embedding the grants economy within the exchange economy. Parents distribute wealth to children, people make donations to charities, migrants remit earnings to families back home, the government of one state makes aid available to that of another, and multilateral development banks provide loans at concessional interest rates. In all instances—though it is best to assume that donors have their own reasons for giving aid and may expect something in return in the future—a grant of economic resources is usually made without an expectation of immediate reciprocity. No one has measured the size of the formal and informal grants economy convincingly, but it is probably huge, and even as the general effectiveness of foreign aid has been questioned, the scholarly literature agrees that sustained postwar grants are necessary and effective to aid violence-afflicted states.[10]

A third type of economy is the appropriation economy. This, too, is characterized by the absence of direct exchange. But whereas the exchange and grants economies are founded, respectively, on voluntary mutual exchange and voluntary unilateral giving, the appropriation economy is based on involuntary taking, that is, coercion. Tax revenue is meant to be expended on public goods and services that benefit the taxpayer, but taxation itself is a form of coercion, as the taxes are taken under threat of punishment for nonpayment. Robbery at the point of a gun is pure appropriation. Between them fall mafia-type and corruption-rife economies: Although the appearance of exchange is maintained—a bribe for a business license or a trading permit, for instance—it is of course a coerced transaction. Exchange encourages production while threat discourages production; at the risk of overly simplifying, if exchange and grants are based on love, appropriation economics is based on fear.[11] The economy of fear is a crucial driver of behavior before, during, and after war and crime and highlights the need to establish a credible and enforceable social contract within, between, and among communities and societies.

Production Possibilities

In exchange economics, a useful visual representation of the productive capacity of an economy and its consumption possibilities is given by what economists call the production possibilities frontier (PPF). For simplicity, let us group all feasible production within an economy into one of two categories of product, such as civilian goods ("butter") and military goods ("guns"). In figure 1.3a, the situation in which all society's resources are used efficiently to produce only civilian goods and no military goods is depicted along the vertical axis at the point where the PPF meets the axis. The situation in which only military goods are produced appears where the PPF meets the horizontal axis. In reality, most societies produce a combination of the two goods, which—if they are being produced efficiently—might be depicted by point A. (Inefficient production would appear as a point beneath the curve.) Economists acknowledge that some military production is necessary, if only for defense. But this comes at the expense of civilian production, as in the move from point A to point B in figure 1.3a. Such a move might happen during periods of heightened conflict, when military expenditure increases, shifting resources toward producing military goods and services. Figure 1.3b indicates what happens if war breaks out, people are injured or killed, and physical capital—buildings, seaports, other equipment—is damaged or destroyed: The overall productive capacity of society shrinks and the entire PPF shifts inward, back toward the point of origin, so that the highest production and consumption points attainable are lower than before. This is how GDP declines in violence-afflicted countries.

> The **production possibilities frontier** shows the maximum possible levels that can be produced of a set of goods and services, given currently available levels of labor, capital, and other production inputs.

The Bathtub Theorem

As consumption depends on production, production in turn depends on the underlying assets that make production possible. One way of seeing this point comes from the bathtub theorem, which says that "the rate of accumulation is equal to the rate of production less the rate of consumption."[12] The inflow of water into the tub represents production; the outflow through the drainpipe represents consumption. If production is greater than con-

FIGURE 1.3. Production Possibilities Frontier for Civilian and Military Goods

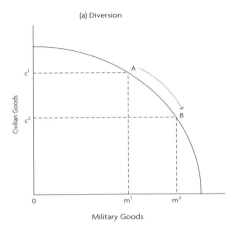

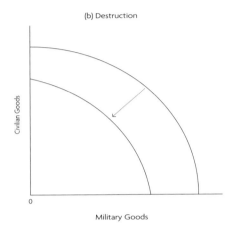

Source: Anderton and Carter (2009)

Bathtub theorem: The inflow of water into a bathtub represents production and the outflow represents consumption. An excess of inflow of production over outflow of consumption adds to the stock of available goods. Conversely, an excess of consumption over production diminishes the stock.

sumption, water accumulates in the bathtub, representing saving. This saving is an asset, a stock of value. In times of crisis, such as war, when production fails, one has to drain part of the stock—slaughtering cattle or eating seeds needed for the next sowing season—to maintain consumption at the accustomed level. A viable reconstruction strategy thus must emphasize rebuilding the stock of assets, that is, having production exceed consumption again. Somehow, the water faucet needs to be turned back on.

Assets and Income

Income, like production, is based on and derived from an underlying base of assets, or capital. A farmer cannot earn income unless the land is fertile, a doctor cannot heal effectively without medical supplies, and a cabinet-maker needs tools to ply his trade. Assets can refer to physical capital, such as machinery, equipment, or physical structures and facilities that one can work with. The planet's natural capital includes raw materials that can go into production processes, some renewable, some not. Assets also encom-

Assets: To produce goods and services, a society needs assets with which to produce. These include natural, physical, human, and social or institutional capital. *Asset stripping* refers to the depletion of the stock of capital to serve current consumption needs, thereby diminishing society's capacity to produce in the future.

pass human capital: people's talents, ingenuity, skills, training, education, knowledge, and experience.

In addition to physical and human capital, scholars have proposed the still controversial notion of social capital, for which there exists neither agreed definition nor measurement. The term roughly refers, however, to an economic asset that consists of the social and communal networks humans build. While it is often used in the context of explaining, for example, the value of civic engagement or the support networks immigrant communities create for themselves, the concept appears in more tangible ways as well. Bank notes may be physical objects, but their function wholly relies on a network of mutual trust among strangers to accept little bits of colored paper as payment in exchange for goods and services. Social capital, too, is a stock of achievements that, once destroyed, can be extremely difficult to rebuild: Trust, once broken, can lead to a complete stop in economic activity and trade.

Social capital: an economic asset consisting of the social and communal networks humans build.

The quantity and quality of assets contribute to production and the productivity of the population and, hence, to their income. As Kenneth Boulding—a renowned economist in his time—has argued, "Essentially, the economic problem of reconstruction is that of rebuilding the capital of society."[13] Of course, many poor communities have little to rebuild in the first place, so the task lies as much in the building as in the rebuilding of the capital or asset base. Policymakers, however, regrettably tend to prioritize income over asset building, meaning that this income may be generated by further depleting the remaining assets. Called asset stripping, recourse to this scheme must be avoided. For example, to generate income, a rural family may decide to slaughter its cattle to sell meat, hides, and other useful parts. By depleting assets, the family generates income but is left poorer. If it is a matter of survival, this is understandable, but ultimately it is a strategy for ruin, not progress.

> The objectives of macroeconomics are low inflation, low unemployment, smooth business cycles, sustainable developmental growth, and policy coordination across political jurisdictions.

Macroeconomic Policy and Politics

The Objectives of Macroeconomics

Five major objectives of macroeconomic policy are low price inflation of inputs, outputs, and assets; low levels of unemployment and high levels of capital utilization; smooth rather than erratic business cycles; sustained and sustainable human development and economic growth;[14] and economic policy coordination across political jurisdictions. The first two objectives, while self-evident, can be stymied by measurement problems. Even in peacetime, many developing economies find it difficult to provide adequate data collection and statistical services to measure aspects of formal and informal labor markets (e.g., population growth, schooling rates, labor force participation, child labor), prices of daily necessities and financial assets (e.g., food and energy costs; land, property, and housing values), and movements of financial capital in and out of a country. A war can interrupt these measurements or even destroy a country's capacity to measure, requiring well-directed and well-focused postwar capacity-rebuilding efforts. Economic theory and, sadly, many economic practitioners often simply assume that the institutions to provide the entire panoply of such measurements are fully functional. In practice, this is often not the case.

Economic Policies and Philosophies

A policy is a set of rules, directions, or guidelines to be followed for a particular issue area. Ideally, government policies are coherent and coordinated so that the many agencies charged with implementing the policy are working toward a common goal. In practice, policy is frequently not well coordinated, nor is it always well executed even if coordinated, and vested interests—domestic and foreign—seek to influence policy to push their own agendas.

Economic growth policy focuses not so much on asset growth itself as on the growth in asset productivity and subsequent income generation. This involves policy areas as disparate as property rights, land reform, education policy, and business regulation, trade, and tax policy, as all of them can help

A *policy* is a set of rules, directions, or guidelines to be followed for a particular issue area. *Economic growth* policy focuses primarily on productivity growth, long-term opportunities for production, and income generation, and less on distribution and consumption. It assumes more of a constitutional and quantitative character. In contrast, *economic development policy* is more concerned with qualitative and equity aspects of the economy, such as rural development; the well-being of women, youth, and the elderly; and minority or disadvantaged populations. This may include measures of personal happiness, community vitality, and resilience.

or hinder the rebuilding of assets and income generation. International financial organizations (IFOs) or multilateral development banks (MLDBs), such as the IMF and the World Bank Group (WBG), have often been seen to push a particular version of growth policy—for instance to liberalize business regulations, open markets to global competition, and minimize government taxation and expenditure. Yet growth issues cannot be divorced for long from distributional issues, that is, how many people are seeing the benefits of economic growth in their own lives. Broad-based economic development policy, rather than economic growth policy, involves urban and rural development; health, education, and personal security; and the concerns of women, youth, the elderly, and other vulnerable populations. Some would include measures of personal happiness and community vitality and resilience as well.[15] As growth helps to finance development objectives, it cannot be ignored.

Macroeconomic Frameworks

There is often disagreement over what macroeconomic framework a country should adopt to meet its economic growth and development goals. Macroeconomics is a contested field, not only among academics but also among policymakers, who jostle for power to implement their vision of how the economy should be handled. Recognizing the need to deal with problems as they emerge, macroeconomic stability involves a delicate dance to achieve sustainable developmental growth. Growth without development is dangerous; development without growth is illusory. Both must be conducted within the parameters of ecological constraints. Figure 1.4 illustrates our view. Short-run economic stabilization may be viewed in an instrumental fashion, as doing what is needed to prevent the economic ship from capsizing—though if one needs to stabilize constantly, perhaps it is because the long-run economic

FIGURE 1.4. Macroeconomic Framework

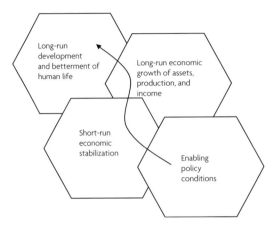

compass is continuously directing the economy into the nearest storm. As for growth, depleting assets to generate current income, as may happen by relying excessively on exploiting mineral wealth, is not a recipe for long-run development success. It leaves a country overly vulnerable to commodity price fluctuations on the world market, requiring overly frequent short-run adjustments and making development and betterment of human life more difficult.

Thus a set of enabling policy conditions is needed, along with criteria to evaluate the success or failure of policy conditions, economic stabilization, economic growth, and human development. Enabling conditions—frequently destroyed in war—refer, for example, to well-functioning, transparent policymaking and policy-implementing institutions, to well-trained and accountable officials, and to a predictable regulatory framework. Because economics is not an end in itself but an instrument directed toward a purpose, the criteria have to do with objectives such as secure lives, decent work, sufficiency of income, ecological sustainability, and justice and human rights. In design and in implementation, macroeconomic policies need to be evaluated—indeed, audited—according to these larger goals.[16]

Sustainable developmental growth suggests that growth without development is dangerous; development without growth, infeasible. Growth must serve developmental purposes and be ecologically sustainable. *Enabling policy conditions* include well-functioning, transparent policymaking and policy-implementing institutions, well-trained and accountable officials, and a predictable regulatory framework.

TABLE 1.1 The Millennium Development Goals

1. Eradicate extreme poverty and hunger
2. Achieve universal primary education
3. Promote gender equality and empower women
4. Reduce child mortality
5. Improve maternal health
6. Combat HIV/AIDS, malaria, and other diseases
7. Ensure environmental sustainability
8. Develop a Global Partnership for Development

Source: United Nations, *The Millennium Development Goals Report 2009* (New York: United Nations, 2009).

The Nexus of Violence, Economic Development, and Global Public Policy

On September 8, 2000, the United Nations General Assembly (UNGA) adopted the United Nations Millennium Declaration,[17] part of which coalesced into the Millennium Development Goals (MDGs) to be achieved by the year 2015 (see table 1.1). Sadly, even though the resolution prominently speaks of peace, security, and disarmament, the MDGs themselves are wholly uninformed regarding the effect of war and violence on poverty and the other MDG goals. They reflect an appalling lack of comprehension that so long as there is violence, there will be no development. Only in August 2009 did the UNGA recognize that virtually every one of the eight MDGs relies on the reduction or cessation of violence:

> Although the linkage between armed violence and development is not explicit in the Millennium Development Goals, they offer entry-points for development agencies to consider. Objectives such as reducing poverty, ensuring maternal health and promoting education are all associated with effective armed violence prevention and reduction initiatives. *Nevertheless . . . there is no Millennium Development Goal that specifically deals with conflict, violence and insecurity.*[18]

The World Bank's *World Development Report 2011* points out that not a single low-income country afflicted by violence has achieved even one of the eight goals.[19] For an illustration, consider Ethiopia. Using GDP data from the Penn World Table project, adjusted for inflation, population growth, and purchasing power differences across countries, figure 1.5 shows a steady rise in GDP from 1950 to 1974. Measured in international or purchasing power parity dollars (I$), Ethiopia's per capita GDP was

FIGURE 1.5. Ethiopia, 1950–2009

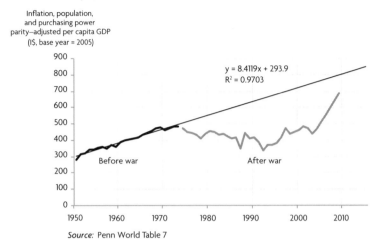

Source: Penn World Table 7

I\$279 in 1950 and I\$473 in 1974, an increase of about 70 percent over 25 years, or 2.8 percent per person per year. In 1974 a violent revolution occurred. In 1977 a war was started with Somalia over the Ogaden region. In the early 1980s several massive famines occurred in part because of a brutally repressive political regime that pursued hurtful economic policies. In the early to mid-1990s violently contested elections took place and long-running secessionist movements in Tigray and Eritrea resulted in more violence. Eritrea gained independence in 1993, but a border war with Ethiopia broke out in 1998 that was only nominally settled in 2000.

Figure 1.5 shows the economic result of Ethiopia's history of upheaval and violence. Over the thirty-year period from 1975 to 2004, economic output per person completely stalled. Had Ethiopia continued to grow at its 1950–74 rate—indicated by the linear trend line in the figure—average production could have reached about I\$800 in 2009 instead of the I\$684 actually achieved, and it reached this level only due to a growth spurt in the last five years of the data series. As in figure 1.2, the area between the trend line and the actual GDP line denotes the size of the cumulative loss of production: I\$7,721, or over eleven years' worth of 2009 income.

Nicaragua is an even more stunning example (figure 1.6). Again measured in international dollars, its per capita production grew from I\$1,948 in 1950

International dollars (I\$): an artificial measure created to make the purchasing power of currencies comparable across countries.

FIGURE 1.6. Nicaragua, 1950–2009

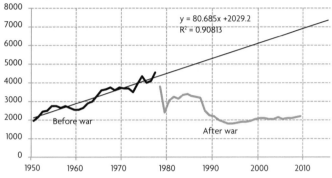

Source: Penn World Table 7

to I\$4,554 in 1977, or about 4.8 percent per person per year, a significant achievement despite a repressive political regime. A long-running revolutionary campaign finally gained traction in 1978 and came to power in 1979, provoking an undeclared proxy war with the United States that involved harbor mining, arms smuggling, and the clandestine support of counterrevolutionaries by the U.S. administration against the express wishes of Congress. An internal war continued until multiparty elections were held in Nicaragua in 1990, resulting in the revolutionaries' electoral defeat. As figure 1.6 shows, by then the economy had completely collapsed, resulting in production per person of only I\$2,192 in 2009—almost equal to the level of I\$2,148 in 1951. The trend line projection suggests that average production without conflict would have reached nearly I\$7,000 by 2009. In other words, in the sixty years from 1950 to 2009, Nicaragua's economy has not grown at all. The reasons for the continued economic stagnation even after the 1990 multiparty elections have to do with the lack of supportive political framework conditions. Former president Arnoldo Alemán (1996–2001) was convicted of embezzlement, money laundering, and corruption and sentenced to a twenty-year prison term—and this by his presidential successor, Enrique Bolaños (2001–06), of the same political party. The former rebel leader, Daniel Ortega, was reelected to the country's presidency in 2006.

Nonwar-related homicide can also severely damage an economy, as the example of the Dominican Republic shows (figure 1.7). Again, the base data

FIGURE 1.7. Dominican Republic, 1950–2009

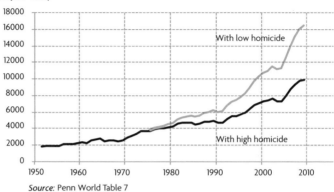

Inflation, population,
and purchasing power
parity–adjusted per capita GDP
(I$, base year = 2005)

Source: Penn World Table 7

on inflation and purchasing power–adjusted per capita GDP are taken from the Penn World Table (version 7). The black line in the figure shows steady production growth from I$1,820 in 1951 (the datum for 1950 is unavailable) to I$9,911 in 2009, or production growth of 7.5 percent per person per year— an impressive achievement, almost on par with India's and China's recent economic growth records. And yet, a study by the United Nations Office on Drugs and Crime estimated that since 1975, growth could have been increased by an additional 1.7 percent per person each year if homicide rates in the Dominican Republic could have been halved from over 16 per 100,000 people to Costa Rica's rate of about 8 per 100,000 people.[20] Using this information, the blue line in figure 1.7 plots the hypothetical per capita GDP levels that the Dominican Republic might have achieved each year. The hypothetical suggests that, by 2009, average production could have been around I$16,456 rather than the around I$10,000 actually achieved, more than a 60 percent difference.

The World Bank concludes rightly that "violence is a major impediment to development."[21] Violence prevention, or at least mitigation, and postviolence reconstruction of a stable social contract are necessary conditions for development: To repeat an earlier point, without peace there is no development. By the same token, lack of development or even the hope for it is a prime cause of violence. A proper macroeconomic framework and policy orientation is thus one important ingredient in the policy mix needed to lower the incidence of violence.

That said, violence rarely permeates the whole of a society. Often it is highly localized, consistently affecting some city neighborhoods more than others or some districts or provinces more than others. However, it can also move from one place to another, sometimes in response to policy action. It is widely acknowledged that Colombia's drug-related violence abated in the 2000s, partly because concerted efforts by its government, with overseas assistance, made it suitable for drug gangs to move to Mexico. There, it is now also acknowledged, Mexican government countermeasures have led to an explosion of violence since 2006, which has led to bases for narcotics trafficking being set up in El Salvador, Guatemala, and Honduras—that is, in countries with weaker systems of law and order. Moreover, "between 1998 and 2005, the United States deported nearly 46,000 convicted felons to Central America, in addition to another 160,000 illegal immigrants," presumably greatly facilitating recruitment for the illicit drug trade.[22] This suggests economically simple, but developmentally highly relevant, substitution effects that only coordinated global public policy can ultimately address.

A diverse economic research literature shows that news of violence can drive foreign direct investment (FDI) and tourists away, even from regions of a country that are completely safe for business, suppliers, employees, and customers to operate and live in. As the saying goes, one bad apple can spoil the barrel. To help mitigate this problem, more fine-grained information on the location, extent, and actual (rather than imagined) danger posed by violence to outsiders needs to be collected and provided. With geographic information systems (GIS) and real-time mapping systems this is not overly difficult to do.[23]

FAILURE AND SUCCESS: Two Case Studies

FAILURE: EL SALVADOR

In 1979 El Salvador fell into a prolonged civil war that lasted until 1991. As tens of thousands of people died and many more fled, the population count in the country actually decreased, as it did in Cambodia during the worst excesses of the Khmer Rouge regime in the 1970s. Since the end of the civil war, violence and insecurity in El Salvador have not ceased. An initial surge of recovery in terms of real per capita GDP (measured in I$) proved short-lived (see figure 1.8). A World Bank country brief reported homicide levels of 55 per 100,000 people in 2006 and a gang culture that impeded the safety of schools, lowered property values, reduced social capital, made travel

FIGURE 1.8. El Salvador, 1950–2009

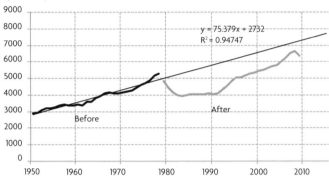

Source: Penn World Table 7

on public transportation to places of employment unsafe, and projected an image of the country that undermined attempts to attract FDI.[24]

A 2005 UNDP study in Spanish and not well known outside the country concluded that the economic cost of violence and insecurity amounted to 11.5 percent of 2003 GDP. Costs include those imposed on the medical sector, absenteeism and productivity losses in the workplace, and legal costs. The losses are more than double what the state expends on the health and education sectors combined. From 1993 to 1997 homicide rates well exceeded 100 per 100,000 people; by the early 2000s they had dropped to a fairly consistent but still extraordinarily high ratio of 60 per 100,000; the WHO considers a rate above 10 per 100,000 epidemic. As elsewhere, homicidal violence primarily has affected young males and differs by day of week and across regions within the country, with homicide rates in 2003 ranging from 10.4 to 54.2 per 100,000 across the country's fifteen administrative regions. The correlation between homicide rates and homicides committed by firearms is very high, a finding that holds for other countries as well.

Ordinary homicide—premeditated or in sudden anger—is but one form of violence and, in 2003, accounted for only 7.2 percent of reported cases of crime against property or persons. Vehicular homicide in El Salvador is also among the very highest per 100,000 people in Latin America and in the world. Intrafamily and sexual violence levels are very high as well. All this suggests that constructive or at least nondestructive social behavior—

as an example of social capital and social contract—has broken down in the face of institutional and society-wide incapacities. A culture of impunity has arisen, and with it, insecurity and consequent failure in the ability to be economically active or productive. In a 2001 survey of business obstacles in Latin America, El Salvador received the most unfavorable scores on crime and organized crime, which were also the greatest among all eleven obstacles countries could be ranked on. Various surveys of small and large businesses in the country suggest business closure or lack of investment on account of crime. Microenterprises were not as affected, suggesting displacement of formal economic activity into the informal sector. Thus the cumulative effects of a culture of violence reduce government tax revenue even as they increase public purse expenditure.

The case of El Salvador illustrates a number of lessons either not learned or not applied. Its violence crisis is a much more severe economic problem than is any realistically conceivable occasional economic crisis. Assets, especially social capital, have not been rebuilt. Trade has been forced to a large extent into the informal economy. Elsewhere, it is true, one must be careful that informal markets are not destroyed when peace comes, dismantling well-established networks of farmers, artisans, petty traders, and end-users. But in the Salvadoran case, the opposite has happened: Existing formal markets have vanished and now operate underground. Foreign assistance has not been forthcoming, in either magnitude or staying power, to assist the country to rebuild state and social institutions and staff them with adequately trained and paid personnel, a point only recently recognized in the World Bank's *World Development Report 2011*.[25] And lack of development has adversely affected all forms of violence, creating a vicious feedback cycle between violence and underdevelopment. While it is challenging to define failure and success unambiguously, there is no doubt that El Salvador is not a successful case of a civil war that ends in sustained peace.

VARIETIES OF SUCCESS: MALAYSIA AND SINGAPORE

It might be surprising to include Malaysia and Singapore as case studies in a text on violence-afflicted countries. But what appear to be successful economies and polities now—especially in Singapore—were hardly preordained. A British trading post and then a colony from 1824, Singapore was occupied by Japanese forces in World War II, as were various parts of Southeast Asia that were previously British outposts. While Siam (Thailand) remained nominally independent, the French held colonial powers up and down the Mekong River in Lao, Cambodia, and Vietnam (French Indochina), and the Dutch settled themselves in Indonesia, the most prominent territory of the Dutch empire. Portuguese claims in the region were smallish, ranging from Goa in India to Macau in China and East Timor in Indonesia. More weighty were the Filipino islands, first a colony of Spain, then the United States. All in all, Southeast Asia and the islands just offshore are a restive region that has experienced very widespread, severe, and longlasting violence.

In 1946, the Malayan Union was formed, British once again, combining the parts of the Malayan peninsula minus Singapore. After a name change in 1948 to the Federation of Malaya, it became a sovereign state in 1957. Lagging behind, Singapore first became a self-governing state within the British Commonwealth in 1959 before achieving full independence from Britain in 1963. Upon independence, it then joined with Malaya, as well as with Sabah and Sarawak, territories across the sea on the otherwise Indonesian island of Borneo, to be part of the Federation of Malaya. But only two years later, in 1965, Singapore was expelled from the federation and today's constellation of sovereign states emerged, with Singapore as an independent island city-state and Malaysia consisting of peninsular Malaysia and Malaysian Borneo.

In recent years the region has been known primarily for the upheaval in Indonesia—the violence in East Timor (Timor-Leste) and Aceh and the political collapse and resurrection of Indonesian politics after the Asian financial crisis of 1997—and for the communist-inspired revolutionary movements in the southern Filipino islands. But Malaysia has had its share of dicey situations. The Philippines still lay territorial claim to Sabah. Indonesia was never happy with large parts of Borneo in foreign hands, and it and Malaysia engaged in political and armed confrontation from 1963 to 1966, which ended only when Indonesia's Suharto took power in a coup against Sukarno. On the Malaysian peninsula itself, there are ethnic tensions among Malays, Chinese, and other cultural-linguistically identified communities. In addition, the Malayan Emergency, as the British called it, or the Anti-British National Liberation War of the post–World War II 1950s that eventually ended with Malaysian independence, was in the main driven by Marxist-Leninist-Maoist-inspired ideology. Although defeated in 1960, a resurgent movement was active on the peninsula, especially in the northern part, from 1968 to 1989 and commanded government attention and diversion of resources.

In all the turmoil regarding the peripheral and interior areas of Malaysia, Singapore sat, independent and with a tradition-laden great harbor

FIGURE 1.9. Singapore (1960–2009) and Malaysia (1955–2009)

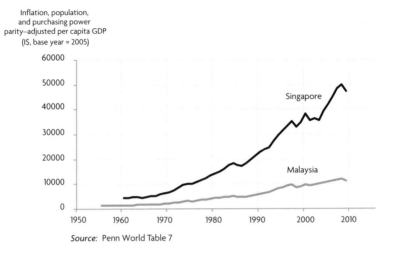

Source: Penn World Table 7

overlooking the Singapore Strait, the strategic waterway between the South China Sea, the Gulf of Thailand, and the Indian Ocean. Figure 1.9 shows the comparative economic records of Malaysia and Singapore. Malaysia's record appears diminished only because Singapore's is so astounding. As figure 1.10 demonstrates, among its immediate other neighbors, Malaysia has performed the best, even as Indonesia, the Philippines, Malaysia, and Thailand all sported roughly comparable per capita GDP levels in the 1950s.

Malaysia and Singapore heeded several of this chapter's lessons. On the whole they avoided, prevented, or mitigated violent conflict. Focusing on physical and human asset rebuilding, they successfully kept an overall, especially distributional, development goal in mind, and with its port, Singapore especially, but later also Malaysia, emerged as peaceful trading economies, attracting plenty of FDI and tourism business. Although Malaysia deals with some unrest and disputes in its peripheral regions to this day, it built on the strengths of its core without wholly neglecting other regions.

Policy Lessons and Tips

LESSON 1.1: Crises of violence are a much more severe economic problem than is the occasional economic crisis.

FIGURE 1.10. Select Southeast Asian Countries, 1950–2009

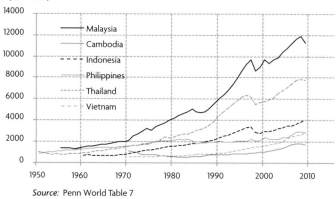

Inflation, population,
and purchasing power
parity–adjusted per capita GDP
(I$, base year = 2005)

Source: Penn World Table 7

LESSON 1.2: Avoid, prevent, and mitigate violent conflict, as heightened tensions, war, and violence always carry adverse economic consequences. Postviolence reconstruction is far more expensive than is prevention.

LESSON 1.3: Build or rebuild assets; do not deplete them. In postviolence reconstruction, the short-run need to address income generation, wealth distribution, and consumption should never detract from focusing on assets.

LESSON 1.4: One cannot manage without managers. Capacity (re)building of institutions and personnel to design and implement proper economic policy is crucial.

LESSON 1.5: One cannot manage without data. Decide on a sequence in which data collection and analysis services can be reestablished.

LESSON 1.6: Consider the elements of the macroeconomic framework broadly and holistically. Do not lose sight of the purpose that economics is to serve. Growth without development is dangerous; development without growth is illusory.

LESSON 1.7: As a rule, peaceful economies are trading economies, and vice versa. Restoring and promoting internal and external trade is vital.

LESSON 1.8: A lack of development affects all forms of violence, and vice versa. An appropriate macroeconomic framework and policy orientation can mitigate violence. Inappropriate policy can worsen it.

LESSON 1.9: Violence can overwhelm country-specific capacity and may require regional or global public policy intervention. Sustained aid to violence-afflicted states is necessary and effective. It has to be structured with peacebuilding and peace maintenance specifically in mind.

LESSON 1.10: Without neglecting violence-rife areas, build the strengths of relatively unaffected regions.

Notes

1. World Health Organization (WHO), *World Report on Violence and Health,* ed. E.G. Krug, L.L. Dahlberg, J.A. Mercy, A.B. Zwi, and R. Lozano (Geneva: WHO, 2002). See Appendix A.

2. The war periods are Cambodia, 1970–91; El Salvador, 1979–91; Guatemala, 1965–95; Mozambique, 1976–92; Nicaragua, 1978–90; Rwanda, 1990–94; and Uganda, 1979–91.

3. R.J. Stohl, M. Schroeder, and D. Smith, *The Small Arms Trade: A Beginner's Guide* (Oxford: Oneworld, 2007), 56.

4. United Nations Development Programme (UNDP), *Post-Conflict Economic Recovery: Enabling Local Ingenuity,* UNDP Bureau for Crisis Prevention and Recovery (New York: UNDP, 2008), 35.

5. For a review of selected literature and scientific issues and criteria to be used in computing the cost of violence, see C. Bozzoli, T. Brück, and S. Sottsas, "A Survey of the Global Economic Costs of Conflict," *Defense and Peace Economics,* vol. 21, no. 2 (2010), 165–176, and C. Bozzoli, T. Brück, T. Drautzburg, and S. Sottsas, "Economic Costs of Mass Violent Conflict: Final Report for the Small Arms Survey, Geneva, Switzerland," Politikberatung Kompakt no. 42, Deutsches Institut für Wirtschaftsforschung (DIW), Berlin, 2008.

6. J. Brauer and J. Tepper-Marlin, "Defining Peace Industries and Calculating the Potential Size of a Peace Gross World Product by Country and by Economic Sector," Report for the Institute of Economics and Peace, Sydney, Australia, 2009.

7. A. Dinar and A. Keck, "Private Irrigation Investment in Colombia: Effects of Violence, Macroeconomic Policy, and Environmental Conditions," *Agricultural Economics,* vol. 16, no. 1 (1997), 1–15.

8. International Monetary Fund (IMF), *World Economic Outlook* (Washington, DC: IMF, April 2011).

9. See, e.g., S.W. Polachek, "How Trade Affects International Transactions," *The Economics of Peace and Security Journal,* vol. 2, no. 2 (2007), 60–68, and literature cited therein.

10. UNDP, *Post-Conflict Economic Recovery; World Bank, World Development Report: Conflict, Security, and Development* (Washington, DC: World Bank, 2011).

11. Adam Smith on self-love in economics: "It is not from the benevolence of the butcher, the brewer, or the baker, that we expect our dinner, but from their regard to their own interest. We address ourselves, not to their humanity but to their self-love, and never talk to them of our own necessities but of their advantages. Nobody but a beggar chuses to depend chiefly upon the benevolence of his fellow-citizens." See A. Smith, *An Inquiry into the Nature and Causes of the Wealth of Nations,* book 1, chapter 2, paragraph I.2.2, available at http://www.econlib.org/library/classics.html (accessed December 6, 2011). Kenneth Boulding (1973) writes about the economics of love and fear. He speaks of three systems: the exchange system, the threat system, and the integrative system. Reactions to threats can take the forms of submission, defiance, counterthreats, fights, or integration of the threatener with the threatened, as when, for example, commonalities between them are established that supersede the threat. To Boulding, grants are one-way transfers, whether made out of love or out of fear. See K.E. Boulding, *The Economics of Love and Fear: A Preface to Grants Economics* (Belmont, CA: Wadsworth, 1973).

12. Boulding, *Economics of Peace,* v.

13. Boulding, *Economics of Peace,* 4.

14. E.F. Schumacher speaks of sufficiency or Buddhist economics, the notion that life satisfaction may well be had from pleasures requiring immaterial inputs rather than material consumption. See E.F. Schumacher, *Small Is Beautiful: Economics As If People Mattered* (New York: Harper & Row, 1973); see also Stiglitz, Sen, and Fitoussi, *Report.* In a similar vein, Kenneth Boulding is a pathbreaker in ecological economics, which views the planet Earth as a closed physical system in which material production absorbs limited natural resources (input) and converts them into waste streams (output). In this view, the part of GDP that measures the monetary value of material production and consumption is nothing more than throughput. To continuously increase material throughput requires a continuous increase in material inputs and consequently a continuous increase in material waste streams, which is physically impossible in a closed system. It follows that economic growth as measured by increases in GDP must be made consistent with raw material use and disposal, so that the integrity of the physical system of the planet can be maintained. Economic growth must be violence-sensitive in terms of human systems but also resource-sensitive in terms of ecological systems. See K.E. Boulding, *Ecological Economics* (Beverly Hills, CA: Sage Publications, 1981).

15. The theoretical and empirical literature on economics and happiness is large. For a (perhaps surprising) review of sorts, see B. Bernanke, "The Economics of Happiness," commencement speech at the University of South Carolina, Columbia, SC, May 8, 2010, available at http://www.federalreserve.gov/newsevents/speech/bernanke20100508a.htm (accessed December 6, 2011). The Organisation for Economic Co-operation and Development (OECD) is championing a worldwide effort to collect, process, and analyze alternative measures of well-being and to introduce them into policymaking. Also see D. Bok, *The Politics of Happiness: What Government Can Learn from the New Research on Well-Being* (Princeton, NJ: Princeton University Press, 2010); and, again, Stiglitz, Sen, and Fitoussi, *Report,* on economic (mis)measures.

16. On macroeconomics and human rights, see, e.g., R. Balakrishnan, D. Elson, and R. Patel, *Rethinking Macro Economic Strategies from a Human Rights Perspective*, Marymount Manhattan College, 2009, available at http://www.networkideas.org/featart/mar2009/MES2.pdf (accessed December 6, 2011).

17. See United Nations Millennium Declaration, UN A/Res/55/2, September 18, 2000, available at http://www.un.org/millennium/declaration/ares552e.pdf (accessed December 6, 2011).

18. UN General Assembly, A/64/228, August 5, 2009, item no. 33, 11. Emphasis added.

19. World Bank, *World Development Report 2011*, xi, 1, 5, 63.

20. United Nations Office on Drugs and Crime (UNODC), *Crime, Violence, and Development: Trends, Costs, and Policy Options in the Caribbean,* report no. 37820 (New York: UNODC, 2007).

21. See World Bank Conflict, Crime, and Violence Team, "Making Societies More Resilient to Violence: A Conceptual Framework for the Conflict, Crime and Violence Agenda," World Bank, Washington, DC, available at http://siteresources.worldbank.org/EXTCPR/Resources/CCV_Framework_Note.pdf (accessed December 6, 2011).

22. World Bank, *World Development Report 2011,* 78.

23. For examples of early work on GIS and violence, see T. Owen and O. Slaymaker, "Toward Modelling Regionally Specific Human Security Using GIS: Case Study Cambodia," *Ambio,* vol. 34, no. 6 (2005), 445–49, and S. Spittaels and F. Hilgert, "Are Congo's Mines the Main Target of the Armed Groups on Its Soil?" *The Economics of Peace and Security Journal,* vol. 4, no. 1 (2009), 55–61.

24. World Bank, "El Salvador Country Brief," available at http://web.worldbank.org/WBSITE/EXTERNAL/COUNTRIES/LACEXT/ELSALVADOREXTN/0,,menuPK:295253~pagePK:141132~piPK:141107~theSitePK:295244,00.html.

25. World Bank, *World Development Report 2011.*

2

LONG-TERM ECONOMIC GOALS
Investment, Productivity, and Growth

On a per capita basis, the average person today is considerably better off than the average person was one hundred years ago. The spatial distribution of that success, however, is unbalanced: Very large numbers of people in Latin America, Africa, and Asia are still poor. Theories of economic growth have to explain both its temporal and spatial dimensions, across and within countries. In identifying the underlying causes of growth, it is helpful to policy if the theory suggests that the causes are endogenous (within the economic system, and thus amenable to policy intervention) rather than exogenous (outside the system, and thus beyond the ability of policymakers to manipulate). New technology that increases labor productivity is regarded as exogenous so long as the mechanism that creates it remains unclear; it is considered endogenous if its development has to do, for instance, with easy access to financial capital, secure property rights, or proper incentive systems.

To move beyond subsistence, an economy needs to generate and sustain a surplus that permits some people to stop working for mere survival and

Endogenous reasons for growth refer to causes that arise from within an economic system and may be amenable to change by policy. *Exogenous* reasons refer to causes seemingly beyond policymakers' influence.

Classical growth theory suggested that any production surplus for the current population would, in time, be consumed by population growth. Societies would repetitively revert to subsistence levels of existence. According to this theory, sustained economic growth per capita was impossible.

take time to experiment, innovate, and implement their ideas. Growth theory in the 1700s and 1800s emphasized the formation and growth of capital, the efficiencies to be gained from specialization, and the advantages of free trade within and across political jurisdictions. Although its distributional aspects are sometimes questioned, to this day free trade remains an important economic doctrine. Regarding capital, classical growth theory also argued that any surplus employed to increase and improve physical capital would bring further surplus but that, in time, population growth would catch up and consume this surplus so that the population would revert to subsistence levels of existence. Under this theory, sustained economic per capita growth was impossible.

With the Industrial Revolution and continued economic growth in the United Kingdom, Western Europe, and North America, it became clear that classical growth theory was wrong about the impossibility of sustained growth. But new growth theories were not formulated until the early to mid-1900s. Two in particular emphasized the roles of technological change and entrepreneurs in fomenting growth. Joseph Schumpeter introduced the now famous phrase of creative destruction: In pursuit of profit, entrepreneurs in a competitive economy bring to market innovative products and processes that, on the one hand, destroy competing lines of business but, on the other hand, are so revolutionary as to move the entire economic system forward.[1] In the transportation sector, the horse and wagon replaced the carrying of goods by hand. Fossil fuel–powered machines replaced water-powered machines. In their time, canals and barges, transoceanic shipping, railroads, the automobile, and modern air travel all transformed prior forms of transportation.

Schumpeter's story was plausible, but the factors driving growth, according to him, were exogenous: They left little room for policy action. The main policy advice was for government to minimize regulatory obstacles to business development. In contrast, Robert Solow's neoclassical growth theory involved a model of a hypothetical economy in which labor, capital, output, growth, investment, technological change, and saving to finance investment were key variables. The endogenous variables in the theory gave some room for policy maneuvers. The theory also led to three predictions:

Neoclassical growth theory focused on the causal relations among factors such as labor, saving, capital, investment, and technological change to predict output and output
growth. *New classical growth theory* has emphasized understanding the institutional
conditions that must be in place to encourage entrepreneurship and make technological change and human capital formation possible. This, in turn, has led to a revival of
long-standing traditions in institutional and evolutionary economics.

first, that an increasing amount of capital per worker—the capital-to-labor
ratio—generates growth because more capital makes workers more productive; second, that countries with an initially small capital-to-labor ratio
would grow faster than those with more capital per worker because each
additional unit of capital would produce a higher return when starting
from low levels than when starting from high levels; and third, that because
of diminishing returns to ever more capital, economies would eventually
reach a steady state, where adding more quantities of capital would generate no additional growth. To overcome the steady state, an economy would
need not only more capital (e.g., more typewriters), but better capital (e.g,
computerized word processors rather than typewriters). In short, neoclassical growth theory suggested that technological change is required for
continuous growth, though the model was silent on just where the change
comes from: Technological change was still exogenous.

Solow's model also predicted that poor countries would catch up to rich
countries. Evidently this did not happen, and economic growth theory
needed to take yet another turn to explain real-world observations.[2] In the
1980s and 1990s Paul Romer, Robert Lucas, and Robert Barro were among
those formulating new classical growth theory. Since then, in addition to
creating models in which technological change is endogenous, theorists
have expanded the definition of capital to include human capital: Unlike
physical capital, which exhibits diminishing returns, it is believed that human capital exhibits increasing returns, meaning that each additional year
of knowledge, education, skill, and experience that workers acquire brings
higher returns than does each prior year. Further, it is possible for people to
share with others the knowledge they have gained at low cost. Thus, economists have focused on systematically identifying the institutional conditions states need to allow innovation, education, and physical and human
capital to flourish. This has led to revived research in institutional and evolutionary economics, which tends to study economies as dynamic and contested social systems. Among these institutions, which may be formal or
informal, are free trade, a minimal regulatory system, sound money, good

law and order—especially secure property rights—and corruption-free government. These make up a panoply of good governance factors that together provide framework conditions permitting private parties to explore Schumpeterian opportunities to better their lives. However, each of these institutions is contested because tweaking the rules can be to the advantage of one party and the disadvantage of another.

Violence disrupts trade and diverts economic resources into unproductive channels. Moreover, it destroys capital and the cultural, political, and economic institutions necessary for good policymaking and implementation, which are necessary also to enhance the endogenous factors of economic growth. But before pursuing the topics of growth-enhancing investment, violence, and economic growth, a few things need to be understood about measuring economic activity.

Measuring Economic Performance

Measuring the Economy Properly

Nominal GDP: GDP not adjusted for the effects of price inflation. *Real GDP:* GDP adjusted for price inflation so that values are comparable across years. A further adjustment for purchasing power differences expresses GDP in international dollars (I$).

The most common measure of economic activity is GDP, usually measured as the money value of all final goods and services produced in a given year. A rising GDP is often associated with greater well-being, but this assumption is problematic, even apart from the distributional concerns mentioned above. Much economic activity goes unmeasured, such as agricultural production for self-consumption or economic activity in illegal markets. Moreover, it is questionable whether some activity that is counted contributes to well-being. Suppose a woman suffers domestic abuse and requires medical treatment. Because treatment results in expenditure and income streams—a payment for medical service received by the attending medical personnel—it is counted as part of GDP. As no intrinsic contribution to well-being is made, perhaps it would be better for GDP not to rise.[3] More nuance may also be needed for military and security-related expenditures that create income for hired personnel and for proprietors and shareholders of security-related companies but that, in the end, merely protect ourselves from ourselves.[4]

TABLE 2.1 Nominal and Real Gross Domestic Product

Year	Nominal GDP	Price Level	Real GDP	Population	Real GDP per capita
1	10,000.0	100.0	10,000.0	100.0	100.0
2	10,500.0	102.0	10,294.1	101.0	101.9
3	11,035.0	104.0	10,596.9	102.0	103.9
4	11,576.3	106.1	10,908.6	103.0	105.9
5	12,155.1	108.2	11,229.4	104.1	107.9

Note: All numbers rounded to one decimal place.

All economic numbers must be adjusted for population growth and output price inflation, especially since the poor tend to suffer the most from inflation (i.e., the devaluation of the purchasing power of money). This involves the concepts of nominal versus real GDP. Suppose that GDP amounts to USD10,000 in year 1 (see table 2.1) and grows between years 1 and 2 by 5 percent—that is, to USD10,500—and then by 5 percent again in each year after. The resulting numbers are referred to as nominal GDP: They are a mixture of quantities produced and the prices at which the quantities are valued, and in our model, they indicate GDP growth by an impressive 21.6 percent in year 5.

But more information is needed to understand the relationship between GDP growth and well-being. We begin with the price level; think of this as an average price across all goods produced. In year 1, let us set the price level at 100 and assume that prices grow by 2 percent each year. Finally, suppose that population grows by 1 percent each year as well. To calculate inflation-adjusted or real GDP, divide any year's nominal GDP by the price level and multiply by 100. For year 5, apart from a small rounding error, we get (USD12,155.1/108.2)*100 = USD11,229.40, meaning that the economy has grown by about 12.3 percent. The word *real* means growth in terms of the monetary value of the number of goods produced, rather than in terms of their prices. But by year 5 the population also has grown, in this case by over 4 percent, so that a further adjustment is necessary. This is shown in the last column of table 2.1. Divide USD11,229.4 by 104.1 to get USD107.9, meaning that real per capita GDP has increased by 7.9 percent. Not bad, but a far cry from the 21.6 percent suggested by nominal GDP growth alone. Only the real GDP and the real GDP per capita numbers are comparable to each other, and the latter is preferred because it also accounts for population growth.

As indicated in chapter 1, when comparing countries using different currencies one more adjustment must be made. Suppose the size of the German economy per person is a hypothetical EUR10,000 and that the size of the U.S. economy per person is an equally hypothetical USD10,000. Further suppose that the euro and dollar exchange on a one-for-one basis (EUR1.0/USD1.0). Thus, translated into U.S. dollars, the value of production per person in Germany is USD10,000. But if the exchange rate changes, say, to EUR1.1/USD1.0, then the size of the German economy—measured in U.S. dollars—appears to be only EUR10,000/EUR1.1 = USD9,091, or about 10 percent smaller. The problem lies not with a shrinking German economy but with a fluctuation in the market exchange rate between the two currencies. To bypass this and other problems with cross-country comparisons, researchers have developed international dollars (I$) or purchasing power parity dollars (ppp-dollars). When analyzing a country over time, GDP and other economic numbers should be adjusted for inflation and population changes; when analyzing across countries, all numbers should additionally be converted to international dollars as well.

Another problem—a big one—is that the monetary size, let alone the growth, of an economy is difficult to measure if a state does not have the labor and institutional resources to properly count the goods and services produced and record their prices. Moreover, in some states the informal economy—made up of economic activity that is neither counted nor taxed—is very large. According to the United Nations Office on Drugs and Crime (UNODC) and Friedrich Schneider (University of Linz, Austria), the six Central American states of Costa Rica, Nicaragua, El Salvador, Honduras, Guatemala, and Panama have shadow economies averaging about half again their reported GDP, and the International Labour Organization (ILO) reports that the share of informal-sector employment in these countries is well above 50 percent of total employment.[5] In Bosnia and Herzegovina, official employment stayed steady at 600,000 people between 1998 to 2005, while informal employment rose from about 200,000 to about 500,000.[6] The United Nations Development Programme (UNDP) speaks of the rise of a "criminal peace economy"[7] that includes, but is not limited to, illegal economic activity, such as trade in narcotics, arms smuggling, human trafficking, or trade in endangered species.

In many war-prone developing countries, especially predominantly agriculture-oriented economies, the informal economy is the economy for the vast majority of people. Injudiciously trying to convert the informal to the formal—even for the good reason of generating public sector tax revenue—

TABLE 2.2 National Income Accounting

1. C+I+G+(X-M) = Y

2. Y = C+S+T

3. C+I+G+(X-M) = C+S+T

4. I+G+(X-M) = S+T

may only disrupt the family and patronage networks of farmers, artisans, petty traders, and end-users and disable an otherwise functioning system. The stabilizing influence that informal economies can offer should not be overlooked. Misguided intervention that disrupts them can delay peace and generate its own conflicts and attendant violence.[8]

The Effects of Violence on Economic Growth

National Income Accounting

Because one cannot earn what someone else has not expended, when all of an economy's expenditure is added up it must equal all of that economy's income derived from production. Equation (1) in table 2.2 shows that the expenditures that result in income (Y) are made by private households on domestic consumption (C); by firms on domestic investment (I), such as equipment and business facilities, either replacing worn-out items or adding to the existing capital stock; and by government (G), on various public services at national, provincial, and district levels. In addition, when a country exports goods (X), it earns income from foreigners, so that foreigners' spending results in revenue streams that must be added to national income. Conversely, when households or firms import (M) goods from abroad, the resulting expenditure leads to income that accrues to the other countries and must therefore be subtracted from the home country, as it does not add to domestic income.

Equation (2) captures the idea that domestic income (Y) can be used in only three ways: as revenue for taxes (T), household consumption (C), or saving (S). Equations (1) and (2) are equal to each other because both are written in terms of national income, Y, derived from and expended on what has been produced. Thus, the next equation repeats the left-hand side of the first equation and the right-hand side of the second one. Because consumption (C) appears on both sides of equation (3), its effect cancels out in terms of national income accounting. We are left with equation (4), which,

TABLE 2.3 Hypothetical National Income Accounting Numbers

5.	I	$= S + (T - G) - (X - M)$
S1:	30	$= 40 + (30 - 30) - (30 - 20)$
S2:	30	$= 30 + (30 - 30) - (30 - 30)$
S3:	30	$= 20 + (30 - 30) - (20 - 30)$
6.	$(I - S)$	$= (T - G) - (X - M)$
S1:	$(30 - 30)$	$= (30 - 30) - (30 - 30)$
S2:	$(30 - 30)$	$= (30 - 40) - (30 - 40)$
S3:	$(30 - 30)$	$= (30 - 20) - (30 - 20)$
7.	$(X - M)$	$= (S - I) + (T - G)$
S1:	$(30 - 30)$	$= (30 - 30) + (30 - 30)$
S2:	$(30 - 30)$	$= (30 - 40) + (30 - 20)$
S3:	$(30 - 30)$	$= (30 - 20) + (30 - 40)$

when rearranged in three different ways, forms the basis for three very important insights. To illustrate these insights, it is useful to associate each of the variables with hypothetical numbers (see table 2.3) and to insert them into equations (5), (6), and (7), respectively.

For equation (5), the numbers assume that government expenditure (G) equals government tax collection (T) so that there is neither a government budget surplus (T > G) nor a government budget deficit (T < G). Equation (5) then tells us how gross private domestic investment (I) on the left-hand side of the equation is financed by the items on the right-hand side. There are three sources: private domestic sector saving (S), government sector saving (T − G), and foreign sector saving (X − M). The first two, private and government saving [S + (T − G)], are also known as national saving. Since, by assumption in this case, the government sector shows neither a budget surplus nor a budget deficit, no government sector savings are generated that could be recycled toward investment, but neither does the government sector absorb savings from the private sector to finance a government budget deficit.[9]

Based on equation (5), table 2.3 displays three scenarios (S1, S2, S3), each of which assumes that investment equals 30. Scenario 1 (S1) assumes

Private domestic saving plus *government sector saving* amounts to *national saving.* This plus *foreign sector saving* finances *gross private domestic investment.*

that private sector saving equals 40. The excess of saving over investment must go, or come from, somewhere. Because it does not finance a government deficit (i.e., T – G = 0), the funds must be related to activity in the foreign sector, in particular the excess of exports (funds flowing into the economy) over imports (funds flowing out). The funds flowing into a country because of exports are foreign currency earnings, and the only way to use them is to return them as investments in the countries from which the currencies are earned.[10] Thus, gross private domestic investment in the home country is unaffected. In scenario 2, part of the former saving of 40 is employed to finance higher import levels. Now the government and the foreign sectors both are balanced, and gross private domestic investment is fully financed from private domestic saving. Finally, in scenario 3, the shortfall of private domestic saving of 20 to finance gross private domestic investment of 30 is made up by the foreign sector. Here the excess of imports over exports means that funds are leaving the country, but the only place where foreigners who earn these funds can reinvest them is in the country from which they come. These will become gross private domestic investment, but the ownership of the assets bought belongs to foreigners (see also the balance of payments discussion in chapter 4).

The three scenarios for equation (6) highlight another aspect of national income accounting. In S1, everything is balanced. But in S2, there is a government budget deficit (T – G = 30 – 40 = –10). Since private domestic saving and the investment sector are in balance, the government budget deficit must be financed from abroad. In this case, the excess of imports over exports results in foreigners holding funds that they lend back to the government of the originating country. In S3, the government budget surplus implies just the opposite, namely, that there must be a trade surplus as well. Think of the three elements of the equation—the private, government, and foreign sectors—as a three-chambered balloon filled with air and tied off. When one squeezes the balloon at one end and the second end is closed off, then the air must move to the third end.

Finally, there are the three scenarios for equation (7). In each, we assume that the foreign sector is balanced. In S1, this is because the domestic and government sectors are balanced as well. In S2, the government budget surplus of 10 can be used to finance the excess of domestic investment over the availability of private sector saving. And in S3, a government budget deficit absorbs a portion of private sector saving so that less is left over to finance gross private domestic investment.

Violence-afflicted states generally suffer from three simultaneous problems, reflected in the national-income accounting equations. First, domestic production falls, so that tax revenue falls even as there is greater need for government expenditure. This results in falling government budget surpluses or, more realistically, in rising deficits (T < G). Second, exports tend to fall off and reduced local production needs to be made up by imports. Thus, the foreign sector becomes unbalanced (X < M). In terms of equation (5), we might have the following scenarios:

$$I \quad = S + (T - G) - (X - M)$$

$$
\begin{aligned}
S1: \quad & 30 \quad = 30 + (30 - 40) - (20 - 30) \\
S2: \quad & 20 \quad = 20 + (30 - 40) - (20 - 30) \\
S3: \quad & 10 \quad = 10 + (30 - 40) - (20 - 30),
\end{aligned}
$$

where in S1 the outflow of funds from excess imports is used by foreigners to finance the government budget deficit. But because of war or other violence, private sector activity falls. Therefore incomes fall, and the remaining income must be used to finance household consumption, so that less is available for private sector saving to finance private sector investment, as in S2. Put differently, almost no one invests in an economy beset by war. If government instead of borrowing from abroad dips into private domestic sector saving, as in S3, then gross private domestic investment falls even more—the third problem violence-afflicted states face.

Compounding and the Rule of 70

Rule of 70: a guide to compute the approximate number of years it takes for an economy to double in size at a given growth rate.

Among the dynamics of growth are its compounding effects. One dollar invested at an annual interest rate of 1 percent will become I$1.01 a year later. The same logic holds for a growing economy. The rule of 70 approximates how long it will take an economy to double in size, given a percentage growth rate. According to the rule, if an economy is growing at 2 percent per year, it will double in about 70/2, or thirty-five years (the exact number of years is thirty-six). Similarly, if an economy grows at 3 percent each year, then it doubles in 70/3, or about twenty-three years, a saving of twelve years of time. Seemingly small differences in growth rates accu-

FIGURE 2.1. Effect on GDP of a Violence-Afflicted State, 1980–2015

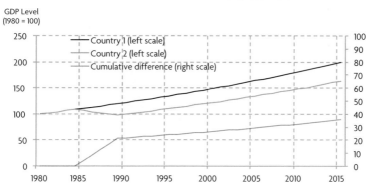

FIGURE 2.2. Cumulative GDP Losses of a Violence-Afflicted State, 1980–2015

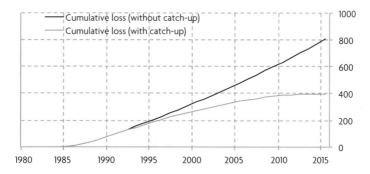

mulate rapidly to substantial differences in average living standards. Some East Asian economies have grown recently by 8 percent per year, so that their economies can double in size in about nine years' time.

Figures 2.1 and 2.2 illustrate the compounding effect in violence-afflicted states. In the first figure, each of two countries starts in 1980 at a GDP level of 100, and each then grows at 2 percent per year. But from 1985 to 1989, country 2 suffers a five-year-long war, with an annual 2 percent GDP decline, whereas country 1 continues to grow at 2 percent per year. From 1990 onward, both countries again grow at 2 percent annually. Using the scale on the right-hand side, the bottom line in figure 2.1 shows that the diverging growth between the two countries during the five-year war amounts to about 22 percentage points. But because of compounding, this is not a one-off effect limited to the war; the difference keeps growing afterward. By the end of one generation—twenty-five years after the war—country 1's GDP stands at 200, whereas country 2's GDP stands at only 163.7, a 36.3-point difference.

Figure 2.2 shows the cumulative GDP losses for country 2 relative to country 1. When both countries grow at 2 percent per year in peacetime, the five-year war interruption amounts, by 2015, to eight times the starting GDP (the cumulative loss is 809.1). For country 2 to catch up to country 1 within twenty-five years of the war's end, by 2015, it would have to grow at a rate of 2.8 percent per year—that is, 40 percent faster (2.8/2.0 = 0.4, or 40 percent) than country 1. Figure 2.2 shows that by the time country 2 does catch up, its cumulative GDP loss during the catch-up time still is nearly four times its starting GDP. Either way, the annual and the cumulative losses are tremendous.

How Collective Violence Perturbs the Economic System

Chapter 1 emphasized the importance of productivity-enhancing investment for long-term economic growth and people's well-being. Investment referred not only to private and public physical capital, such as roads and machinery, but also to human, cultural, social, and institutional capital, such as levels of education, the degree of trust among citizens, and the extent of well-working property rights, contract enforcement, and monetary stability. All of these are vulnerable to the effects of war. But more than investment is at stake. Interpersonal and collective violence can perturb the economic system in a variety of mutually reinforcing ways. Starting with the supply side, war often is associated with spikes in input prices. Raw materials may be harder to get, as suppliers charge higher prices to obtain and transport them. Electricity and other utility services may be disrupted and therefore disrupt other production as well. Laborers and farmworkers may be drafted into armies or become victims or refugees, so that it is more difficult to find qualified workers. New investment to make agricultural or industrial production more efficient is not undertaken for fear that the war will undo the progress. Maintenance of existing equipment may be deferred, leading the machinery to break down earlier. Average production costs rise. Economic growth falls, employment falls, and unemployment rises. The size of the effect depends on the type, intensity, duration, and spatial reach of the violence. The more serious is the violence, the greater the adverse effects.

On the demand side of the economy, all five components of aggregate demand captured in equation (1) can be adversely affected. Demand for consumption falls as people try to save money, anticipating unemployment or expecting a long war. Firms are reluctant to invest. Exports falter as transportation routes, especially airports, seaports, and border crossings, are blocked. As imports cannot continue unabated, people seek recourse to higher-priced domestically produced goods, driving up the cost of living. Government tax revenue, and thus spending, drops as economic activity falls or shifts from the formal to the informal sector. To compensate, a government can try to borrow, increase its debt load, and inject spending, especially military-related spending, into the economy to prop it up. But replacing private economic activity with public activity is not a viable long-term economic strategy. While individual people may see their fortunes rise in war, entire economies do not. Violence creates a vicious cycle that continually depresses the economy.

Institutions and Policies

Three Societies

Every community has three overlapping societies: commercial, civil, and political (or economics, culture, and politics). Commercial society allocates resources through markets, civil society through moral suasion, and political society through power.[11] Most adults are engaged in all three societies simultaneously: They participate in economic life as producers and consumers, engage in civic activities from neighborhood football clubs to membership in global nongovernmental organizations, and participate in public life, if only as occasional voters.

A well-functioning society is also well balanced. Commercial society running rampant without moral checks from civil society and regulatory checks from political society is just as much a recipe for disaster as politics that lets neither commerce nor civil society bloom. All three societies operate in both the domestic and transnational spheres. Local business has its counterpart in transnational business, local NGOs in increasingly prominent transnational NGOs, and the local public sector in international organizations, such as the United Nations, the Association of Southeast Asian Nations (ASEAN), the European Union, or the African Union (AU).

Each actor has its own concerns and objectives, and the outcome of each seeking to influence or trade with the others determines the governance of society, with formal lawmaking, implementing, and enforcing agencies delegated to government. One can argue that a particular role for government or certain conditions for economic growth are ideal. But in practice, one may say that commercial society drives the economy and economic growth, political society provides the framework to direct and manage them, and civil society checks on the quality of the economy, for instance by insisting on subjecting growth to environmental requirements or demands for equitable income distributions.

Usually, institutions and policies are thought of only from the viewpoint of political society. At the national level, ministries of economics, finance, trade, labor, industry, education, and similar realms are charged with implementing policies that their political masters set. Regardless of their specific subject-matter charge and expertise, the ministries must be directed to act in a coordinated fashion toward the goal of rebuilding society's capital. In one sense, all of them are state investment agencies, investing in, say, education, infrastructure, or labor force productivity. After a conflict, commerce, labor, immigration, and finance ministries might need to work jointly on repatriating physical, human, and financial capital that has fled. Returning the diaspora home can rekindle economic growth. Private charities should be welcomed when their work fits into an overall conception of rebuilding, maintaining, and securing the population's well-being. States blessed with abundant natural resources need credible ways of putting aside a portion of the earnings to build endowments that return dividends over the long term, as Timor-Leste (East Timor) did with its petroleum fund, stocked by export revenue from its offshore oil and gas fields. Earnings and withdrawals from the fund can supplement the government budget to finance much-needed infrastructure projects. Sometimes referred to as sovereign wealth funds, states such as Kuwait and Singapore—one natural resource rich, the other not—have had such funds for many years.

Aid, Remittances, Foreign Direct Investment, and Trade

Official development assistance (ODA) reached about USD100 billion in 2006.[12] In contrast, overseas workers' remittances to their home countries amounted to USD300 billion in 2006.[13] FDI reached over USD1 trillion.[14] Truly freeing up global markets for trade probably would result in even larger numbers. When policymakers in violence-afflicted states think about capital rebuilding, they should concentrate not solely on foreign aid but also on reconstituting and sustaining private sector activity. Foreign aid, like military intervention, ultimately reflects third-party interests, and for the recipient country it can thus be capricious, haphazard, and short in duration. The academic community has argued only recently that aid ought to be nonpolitical, predictable, and longlasting, on the order of ten years after conflict,[15] and that it ought to be designed, delivered, and audited specifically with peacebuilding and peace maintenance in mind.

International Financial Institutions

The phrase *international financial institution* (IFI) refers mainly to the IMF and the WBG, but also to regional development banks, such as the African Development Bank (AfDB), the Asian Development Bank (ADB), the Inter-American Development Bank (IADB), and the European Bank for Reconstruction and Development (EBRD). The IMF is engaged in short-term lending to support macroeconomic stabilization. The others are engaged in long-term lending to build or rebuild physical infrastructure and provide social services. The WBG consists of the International Bank for Reconstruction and Development (IBRD), the International Development Association (IDA), the International Finance Corporation (IFC), the Multilateral Investment Guarantee Agency (MIGA), and the Center for Settlement of Investment Disputes (CSID). Both the IMF and the WBG are autonomous organizations, each constituted by international treaties to which states accede when they apply to become members.

The IMF describes itself as "an organization of 187 countries, working to foster global monetary cooperation, secure financial stability, facilitate international trade, promote high employment and sustainable economic growth, and reduce poverty around the world." In practice, three areas dominate its day-to-day work. First, economic surveillance monitors members' economic and financial developments and offers policy advice aimed at preventing crisis. Second, the IMF makes short-term loans to countries with balance-of-payments problems to support policies aimed at correcting underlying difficulties. Third, the IMF provides technical assistance and training. The IBRD and IDA describe their work as providing "low-interest loans, interest-free credits and grants to developing countries for a wide array of purposes that include investments in education, health, public administration, infrastructure, financial and private sector development, agriculture and environmental and natural resource management."[16]

Both the IMF and the WBG, as political entities created by sovereign states, can be constrained in the data they collect and the policy advice they give. Both have been criticized for pushing inappropriate and even harmful policies on member states as conditions for receiving loans. At one time, the World Bank financed a number of large dams for hydropower generation. While power generation and economic growth are obviously related, the dams' construction sometimes displaced vulnerable populations from ancestral lands and damaged the environment. Negotiating infrastructure loans with central government politicians and bureaucrats to generate electric power to be transmitted to faraway cities while leaving local populations uprooted, displaced, and unattended betrayed notions of economic development that civil society rightly criticized. From time to time, the World Bank therefore has had to acknowledge errors and change policy and practice. In the late 1990s, however, the bank also led in promoting research on the economics of armed conflict and translating findings into practical assistance.

FAILURE AND SUCCESS: Two Case Studies

For our case studies, we consider two sets of countries. The first consists of what once was routinely called the European periphery, especially Greece, Portugal, and Spain; the second is the European core, especially France, Germany, and Italy. Together with Belgium, Luxembourg, and the Netherlands, the core countries founded the European Coal and Steel Community (ECSC) with the 1951 Treaty of Paris and the European Economic Community (EEC) with the 1957 Treaty of Rome. The EEC evolved into today's twenty-seven-member European Union.

By the 1950s, the core countries were all democracies. In contrast, the peripheral countries were controlled by military dictatorships and saw severe internal unrest and civil war. Greece was wracked by internal violence for thirty years after World War II. A civil war lasted from 1945 to 1949 and a U.S.-backed coup d'etat resulted in a military junta that ruled from 1967 to 1974. The junta collapsed following student riots in 1973 and Turkey's invasion of Cyprus in 1974. Greece joined what now is the European Union in 1981.

Portugal's last king—Manuel II—was overthrown in 1910. After continual unrest and World War I, a coup d'etat established a dictatorship in 1926, cemented in 1933. Formally neutral in World War II, the country fought a losing series of colonial wars (1961–74) and eventually relinquished all its holdings, including massive territories such as Angola and Mozambique (which then went on to fight their own, longlasting postcolonial internal wars). A democratic regime was introduced in Portugal only in 1976, two years after a revolution that overthrew the generals. Only when Portugal joined the EEC in 1986 did it see a measure of economic stability and integration into a wider market.

Like its peninsular neighbor, Spain was formally neutral in World War II, dealing with the ongoing aftermath of the Spanish Civil War (1936–39). From this, General Franco's forces emerged victorious and a military dictatorship survived until the general's death in 1975. Modern democracy was established with a new constitution in 1978. Spain joined the EEC in 1986. Franco had kept Spain out of the United Nations, though Spain's political and economic isolation ended in 1955 when the United States roped it into its anti-Soviet European bulwark. Shortly afterward the country received IMF assistance and put in place a set of young economic technocrats whose policies pulled off *el milagro español*—the Spanish miracle, which was an economic boom period lasting from 1959 to 1973.

Figure 2.3 shows, perhaps counterintuitively, that all three peripheral countries experienced strong economic growth in the 1950s, 1960s, and early 1970s. Likewise, all three experienced economic stagnation lasting for about a decade after the overthrow of their respective dictatorships and the establishment of modern democracy. The pattern is exactly the same: Strong investment permitted productivity and consumption and hence GDP increases, even under odious political regimes (something we also learn from South Korea and Taiwan under their respective military dictatorships, or Malaysia and Singapore under their "strong" leadership models). But with regime change came investor uncertainty, a decline in investment and productivity, and stagnation in consumption levels, lasting from about the mid-1970s to the mid-1980s.

In 1950 all six countries started at broadly similar per capita GDP levels of I$5,000 (France a bit more; Portugal a bit less) and in 2009, all except Portugal ended at about the same place, I$20,000 of consumption and I$30,000 of GDP. But the occasional recessionary wrinkles notwithstanding, the growth path for the core is steadily upward, whereas that for the periphery is way up, then stagnating, and then way up again. The periods of accelerated progress are tied intimately to the European project initiated by the core. For both Portugal and Spain, after stagnation, economic advancement did not occur again until EU integration. For Greece even that did not help until the post–Cold War mid-1990s, when Bulgaria and Romania opened up, the Balkan wars ended, and Greece prepared for entry into

FIGURE 2.3a. Economic Growth

Greece, 1950–2009

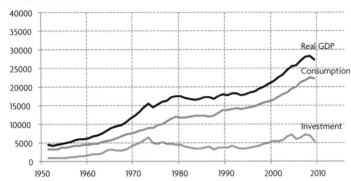

Portugal, 1950–2009

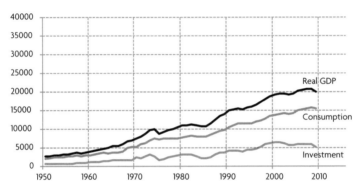

Spain, 1950–2009

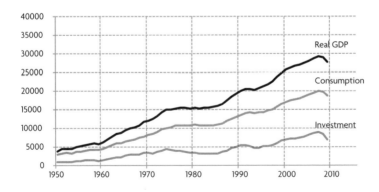

Inflation, population, and purchasing power parity–adjusted per capita GDP, consumption, and investment
(I$, base year = 2005)

Source: Penn World Table 7

FIGURE 2.3b. Economic Growth

France, 1950–2009

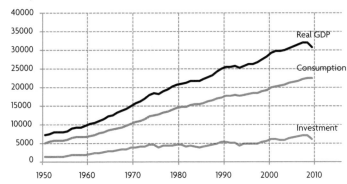

Germany, 1950–2009

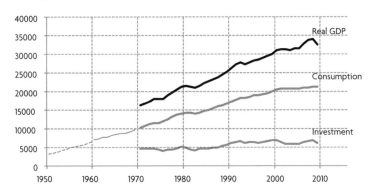

Italy, 1950–2009

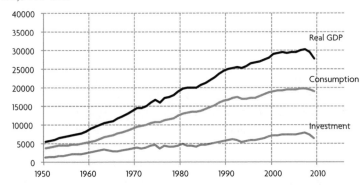

Inflation, population, and purchasing power parity–adjusted per capita GDP, consumption, and investment
(I$, base year = 2005)

Source: Penn World Table 7
Note: Germany, 1970–2009, for 1950–1960 and 1960–1969 computed from http://www.destatis.de/jetspeed/
              portal/cms/Sites/destatis/Internet/EN/Content/Statistics/VolkswirtschaftlicheGesamtrechnungen/
              Inlandsprodukt/Volkseinkommen1950,property=file.xls.

what would become the eurozone as of January 1, 1999. Proximity fosters trade and trade fosters growth. It is probably no coincidence that this periphery, with Ireland, today forms the core of the eurozone financial crisis.

From 1948 to 1951—before the Treaty of Paris—Marshall Plan aid or, officially, European Recovery Program (ERP) aid, was provided in substantial per capita amounts to the three core countries, at least relative to the but trifling per capita amounts provided to Greece and Portugal, and not at all to Spain. The plan's narrow and purely economic effects are debated to this day, but there seems little question that its wider politico-economic, institutional effects were crucial and wide-ranging. Recognizing that Germany again would have to be the hub of the European economy and that all its neighbors would need to rely on a well-functioning Germany economy for their own well-being, the Marshall Plan helped to initiate a pan-European vision for an integrated free trade area, preceding the core's ECSC. Like the IMF's lending today, the Marshall Plan loans were a ready source of foreign exchange to purchase industrial and consumer goods in the United States. The Americans thus tied much aid to their own suppliers back home. But, crucially, each European country had to come up with its own plan for how best to use these resources, a lesson the IMF has only learned in the 2000s. In Germany, repayment of Marshall Plan grant elements for industrial rebuilding and redevelopment was made in local currency into a revolving fund that then would relend, internally and seemingly in perpetuity: Today, the Kreditanstalt für Wiederaufbau (KfW) is still a going concern, long having repaid the initial Marshall Plan seed money.[17]

The West European core also could rebuild on the basis of a highly skilled and educated workforce and, culturally, relatively homogenous populations. It almost literally could pick up the pieces for the simple reason that there were pieces to pick up. By contrast, Spain lost not only half a million people in its civil war but another half million who moved away on account of Franco's fascist regime. Social capital was more severely disrupted there and in the other peripheral countries than in the core. All three peripheral countries also were predominantly agricultural rather than industrial, and despite postwar growth, by 1960, far behind the core in terms of per capita GDP (see figure 2.3), as they would remain for decades.

That said, regional disparities within the core also have caused tension. Italy is perhaps the most famous case, for its advanced north and lagging south. In West Germany, the border region toward East Germany was moribund and excluded from effective economic resurgence. All in all, though, the cases provide some concrete insight into assets and growth issues, particularly regarding the importance of asset and institutional rebuilding; a helpful neighborhood of states with whom to trade; the absence of continual violence; the opening up of political decision-making processes for participation, transparency, and accountability; and sustained, albeit thoroughly self-interested, outside interest and substantial financial and technical aid to spur reconstruction and development. This is the kind of aid that neither El Salvador (see chapter 1) nor the European periphery received after World War II.

Policy Lessons and Tips

LESSON 2.1: Economic growth is necessary and welcome. Always adjust economic growth measures for population growth, output price inflation, and purchasing power differences. Growth compounds quickly; do not forgo even small growth differentials.

LESSON 2.2: National income accounting captures only part of what societies should measure to gauge progress. Supplementary measures of physical and mental well-being should be sought and analyzed in relation to how economic policies help or hinder progress on these scores.

LESSON 2.3: A generally agreed-upon theory of how to make growth happen does not exist. In general, however, government is to set investment-enhancing framework conditions, issue proper laws and regulations, define intervention points, and provide for adequate institutional capacity to implement policy, but otherwise leave the business of growth to the private sector.

LESSON 2.4: Because of its overarching powers, government is contested. A well-functioning society is also a well-balanced one, and political society alone cannot determine economic growth policy. Commercial and civil society are necessary to drive growth and check on its quality. Civil participation, transparency, accountability, and recall of policymakers are important elements in this.

LESSON 2.5: No precise yardstick regarding a long-term economic growth rate to aim at exists. Prewar experiences, the remaining capital stock and plans for rebuilding it, as well as the records of similarly affected and neighboring states, may provide guidance for a reasonable growth rate. Undershooting forfeits advances in living standards.

LESSON 2.6: The pursuit of economic growth at all costs—that is, without poverty and violence reduction strategies—can be self-defeating and plunge a society (back) into war. Both good governance and good government, including capable policy planning, design, implementation, execution, and follow-through, are prerequisites for sustained peace and prosperity.

LESSON 2.7: Violence affects both the supply and the demand sides of an economy. Addressing only one side or, worse, only one aspect of one side, is insufficient. The economic cost of violence is large and, over time, amounts to dramatically large numbers. One of the best long-term investments a society can make is to reduce, prevent, and mitigate violence in all its forms.

LESSON 2.8: As institutions, both the WBG and the IMF have sometimes been late to recognize and acknowledge case-specific circumstances that would have required deviation from standard policy recommendations.

Notes

1. J. Schumpeter, *Capitalism, Socialism and Democracy* (New York and London: Harper & Brothers, 1942).

2. See V. Cerra and S.C. Saxena, "Growth Dynamics: The Myth of Economic Recovery," Working Paper no. 226, Basel, Bank for International Settlements, 2007. They show that developing economies can converge on developed economies so long as they can avoid "wars, [financial] crises, and other negative shocks . . . [that] lead to absolute divergence and lower long-run growth. . . . The output costs of political and financial crises are permanent on average, and long-term growth is negatively linked to volatility" (from abstract). Nonetheless, even if the failure of convergence can be linked to repetitive, severe crises, it still would be useful to identify the endogenous drivers of positive economic growth.

3. On the mismeasure of GDP and the measurement of well-being, see, e.g., Stiglitz, Sen, and Fitoussi, *Report*.

4. Inasmuch as security can be likened to an insurance premium to deal with risk, it is probably proper to include security-related expenditure in GDP. See T. Brück, "An Economic Analysis of Security Policies," *Defense and Peace Economics,* vol. 16, no. 5 (2005), 375–389. But higher risk implies higher premia, and vice versa.

5. See UNODC, *Crime, Violence, and Development,* 84.

6. UNDP, *Post-Conflict Economic Recovery,* 77.

7. UNODC, *Crime, Violence, and Development*, 83–84; UNDP, *Post-Conflict Economic Recovery*, 77–78; see also World Bank, *World Development Report*.

8. See, e.g., J.P. Dunne, "After the Slaughter: Reconstructing Mozambique and Rwanda," *The Economics of Peace and Security Journal*, vol. 1, no. 2 (2006), 39–46, on Mozambique and Rwanda and the literature cited there, especially T. Brück, "The Economics of Civil War in Mozambique," in J. Brauer and K. Hartley, eds., *The Economics of Regional Security: NATO, the Mediterranean, and Southern Africa* (Amsterdam: Harwood, 2000), 191–215.

9. To achieve a balanced government budget is not fancy. In 2011 Chile had a budget surplus of 0.2 percent of GDP, and Estonia of –0.1 percent of GDP, that is, very close to balance. See "Trade, Exchange Rates, Budget Balances, and Interest Rates," *Economist*, available at http://www.economist.com/node/21543568 (accessed January 31, 2012).

10. For example, China earns U.S. dollars from its exports to the United States. Some of these dollars will be used to purchase, say, petroleum from Saudi Arabia. But it does neither China nor Saudi Arabia any good to hoard the dollars. Instead, they mostly will be returned to the United States by purchasing U.S. government bonds or other assets in the United States on which China, Saudi Arabia, and other countries holding dollars earn interest.

11. See J. Brauer and R. Haywood, "Nonstate Sovereign Entrepreneurs and Nonterritorial Sovereign Organizations," in W.A. Naudé, ed., *Entrepreneurship and Economic Development* (Basingstoke, UK: Palgrave Macmillan, 2011), 294–316. An overlap might occur in commercial diplomacy, i.e., joint trade missions by diplomats and business people.

12. For the twenty-two members of the Development Assistance Committee of the Organisation for Economic Co-operation and Development (OECD), see "Development Co-operation Report," summary, OECD, January 2008, available at http://www.oecd.org/dataoecd/21/10/40108245.pdf (accessed December 6, 2011).

13. UNDP, *Post-Conflict Economic Recovery*, 86.

14. See United Nations Conference on Trade and Development (UNCTAD), *World Investment Report 2009*, available at http://www.unctad.org/Templates/WebFlyer.asp?intItemID=5037&lang=1 (accessed December 6, 2011).

15. So has the World Bank; see *World Development Report 2011: Conflict, Security, and Development* (Washington, DC: World Bank, 2011).

16. See http://www.imf.org/external/about.htm and http://web.worldbank.org/WBSITE/EXTERNAL/EXTABOUTUS/0,,pagePK:50004410~piPK:36602~theSitePK:29708,00.html (accessed January 10, 2012).

17. Germany received about USD1.4 billion and repaid an agreed-upon USD1.0 billion under the London Debt Agreement.

3

MACROECONOMIC STABILIZATION
and Dealing with Turbulence

Assets and income are inextricably linked. They rise and fall together; if there are no assets in an economy, there will be no income. But having assets does not guarantee stability. This chapter deals with macroeconomic turbulence and economic statecraft in the short term, bearing in mind that the short and long terms are connected. If an economy can be compared to a ship, then the long term involves choosing the right port as a destination; the short term involves taking the necessary detours to avoid storms. Adopting economic regulations and policies that fail to reassure private investors or threaten to dispossess them is like dismantling the ship on the way to the storm. The bigger the ship, the more comfortable and safe will be the journey, and as size provides intrinsic stability, asset building must relentlessly continue.

Investment-sensitive reform must reassure not only investors but workers and society at large. Reform must be sensitive to conflict as well, particularly the danger of renewed violence. Scholarship and international financial institutions now agree that it is useless to grow the economy at the risk of recreating the conditions that gave rise to violence in the first place. Slow and steady is better than fast and risky. Diverting some resources to peace-building investments, recreating and strengthening the social contract, and

Macroeconomic stabilization policies seek to moderate erratic swings in the business cycle. The tools include fiscal and monetary policy, even though macroeconomic stabilization is not their primary purpose.

reconstructing the framework that supports social stability may at first be more important than building assets to directly enlarge the economy. As UNDP states the current consensus view, "macroeconomic policies must give priority to minimizing conflict risk, even as they promote growth. This may mean tolerating moderate inflation and budget deficits."[1]

A macroeconomic stabilization strategy seeks to moderate erratic movements in the business cycle. Its main tools are fiscal and monetary policy. But the purpose of fiscal and monetary policy is not macroeconomic stabilization. Fiscal policy pertains to the management of public finances, that is, to collecting taxes and disbursing revenue. By setting and changing tax rates and disbursement objectives, certain social and economic goals can be fulfilled, such as income redistribution. Likewise, monetary policy involves maintaining the internal and external purchasing power of a state's currency. Stabilization is a secondary function of both types of policy, and only a few states have the relative luxury to employ fiscal and monetary policy in this manner. In most states—especially violence-afflicted ones—chaotic fiscal and monetary policy contribute to macroeconomic instability and need to be stabilized themselves. They need to be regularized, made less capricious, and be handled more competently. This requires political credibility and technical capacity building.

A Macroeconomic Framework

All segments of society prefer to avoid large swings in business cycles. Households like to be confident of continuous employment and income. Businesses prefer a stable economic environment and stable consumer incomes, as they greatly facilitate planning and reduce risk, especially for large-scale, costly investments. Policymakers favor a stable economic environment because it provides relative surety about the sizes of revenues and expenditures. A country's trade partners prefer stability because when an economy plunges into recession it usually buys less from its overseas partners; also, a country with a volatile economy may be tempted to manipulate its currency's exchange rate. Both can hurt trading partners. In short, everyone agrees on the goal of securing a stable macroeconomic en-

FIGURE 3.1. Aggregate Demand and Aggregate Supply

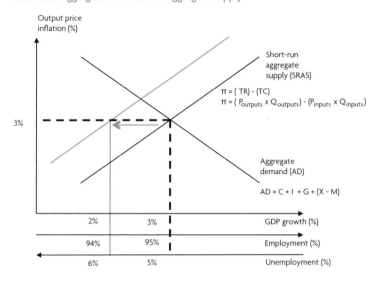

vironment. The disagreements are over the details, mechanics, and effective implementation and timing.

The Short-Run AD/AS Framework

The aggregate demand/aggregate supply framework, or the AD/AS model, is a useful heuristic device for considering questions of fiscal and monetary policy, as it pulls together many relevant demand- and supply-side variables, considers all actors (private and public), integrates domestic and foreign sectors, and simultaneously considers the short and long terms in a single visual representation. Figure 3.1 portrays an economy. The vertical axis denotes inflation (in percentage terms) of the goods and services an economy produces. On the first horizontal axis, economic growth is measured by GDP, also in percentage terms.[2] A second horizontal axis measures employment as a percentage of the labor force. When the employment axis is run the other way, from right to left, one obtains a sense of the size of unemployment, also measured as a percentage of the labor force.

The upward-sloping line in the figure is called the short-run aggregate supply (SRAS); in contrast, long-run aggregate supply (LRAS) refers to an economy's inherent productive capacity—its sheer potential to generate output on account of its asset base—regardless of whether that capacity is

> *Short-run aggregate supply* (SRAS) refers to the business sector supplying goods and services to the economy in response to changes in the market price that can be obtained. *Long-run aggregate supply* (LRAS) refers to an economy's inherent productive capacity—its potential to generate output on account of its asset base—regardless of whether or not that capacity is productively employed or lies idle.

productively employed or lies idle. To see why the SRAS line slopes upward, consider first the black SRAS line and assume that the economy is operating where output price inflation is 3 percent and GDP growth is also 3 percent (with an implied 95 percent employment rate and 5 percent unemployment rate). Suppliers of goods and services are in business to earn profit (Π), that is, total revenue (TR) minus total cost (TC). TR, in turn, is the combination of the prices received times the units of output sold ($P_{output} \times Q_{output}$). Likewise, TC is the combination of prices paid times the units of input needed, such as raw materials and labor ($P_{input} \times Q_{input}$). The argument now proceeds on the assumption—to be relaxed shortly—that the prices of inputs are constant (unchanged). If for any reason the output prices should increase, firms notice an extra profit opportunity because costs with constant input prices are not rising as fast as revenue. A firm will therefore want to produce more output. This makes the supply-line slope upward.

If one makes the opposite assumption about prices, profits are threatened. For example, if input prices rise faster than output prices, then production becomes relatively more expensive, profits decline, and producers make less than they might have intended to. Growth is throttled. This is visually represented in Figure 3.1 by a shift of the entire black SRAS line to the left (from the black to the blue line). Because less is produced, one can read off the horizontal axes that GDP growth is now only 2 percent, employment falls from 95 percent to 94 percent, and unemployment correspondingly rises from 5 percent to 6 percent of the labor force. Input prices or production costs can rise on account of higher regulatory compliance costs, higher raw material costs, higher labor costs, or higher transportation costs. Input prices can also fall, especially when improved technology lowers production costs per unit produced. In that case, the change in short-run aggregate supply shifts the black SRAS line to the right.

Feedback Effect

Changes in an economic system affect participants, who change their behavior, which in turn affects the system. In the case of initially constant output

FIGURE 3.2. Feedback Effect

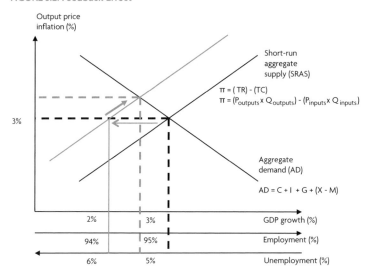

price inflation and more rapidly rising input price inflation (figure 3.1), the reduced production on account of falling profit opportunities means that the existing demand for goods and services cannot be satisfied as well as before. Buyers consequently compete for reduced supply and push output prices up a bit, which in turn stimulates supply a little bit as well (see the switch, in figure 3.2, from the black to the blue situation). When the dynamics have worked themselves out, the economy ends up with output price inflation running at about 3.5 percent, and with GDP growth at about 2.5 percent, employment at 94.5 percent, and unemployment at 5.5 percent.

Aggregate Demand

If short-run supply is primarily a function of profit opportunities and the various revenue and cost factors that affect them, then aggregate demand consists of the summation of demand by various categories of buyers. In the figures, aggregate demand (AD) is written as an equation, the same equation used in chapter 2 for national income accounting: C stands for consumption by private households, I for investment by firms, G for government spending at the federal, provincial, and district or municipal levels, and (X − M) for the net value of exports and imports. The value of exports is added because it represents demand from overseas for domes-

> **Aggregate demand** (AD) refers to the sum of anticipated or actual spending in an economy.

tically produced goods, but the value of imports is subtracted because it reflects demand that is realized in another economy. The AD line slopes downward because the lower is output price inflation, the higher is the incentive to make purchases at home.

If any component on the right-hand side of the AD equation rises in value, then the left-hand side must rise in value also, reflecting more aggregate demand for goods and services. This is shown in figure 3.3 by shifting the black AD line outward toward the right, along the GDP-growth axis, to become the blue AD line. With rising demand relative to available supplies, output prices eventually rise as demand competes for access to the supplies. This signals profit opportunities. More production—and employment—will be forthcoming.

Just Ten Variables

The macroeconomic framework involves just ten variables: output prices, input prices, quantities used and produced (inputs and outputs), GDP, employment, unemployment, consumption, investment, public sector expenditure, and the net value of exports and imports. Astonishingly, just about anything that can happen in the world can be reflected in one or more of these variables, which then affects the economic system. If threat of war induces people to save more, the reduced consumption drags aggregate demand leftward along the GDP growth axis. Reduced demand implies less production and, hence, reduced growth, reduced employment, increased unemployment, and reduced output price inflation as producers eventually lower prices to attract the remaining shoppers (or do not raise prices as much as they might otherwise). All else held constant, reduced consumption means more saving. This means that excess supplies of loanable funds should drive down interest rates and, in turn, encourage investment. But even at low interest rates, firms hesitate to borrow if they, too, fear the onset of war. Government can make up for slackening private demand by borrowing and stimulating the economy through war-related production, but consumption generally falls much more quickly than government can react to pick up the slack, so that an economic slowdown or an outright recession is likely. And, of course, preparing for war is not the preferred way to stabilize an economy.

FIGURE 3.3. Aggregate Demand

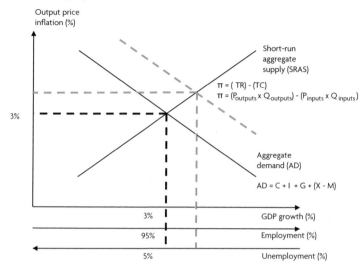

Macroeconomic Objectives

A simple and convenient tool, the AD/AS framework can inform one quickly about causes, pressures, dynamics, and consequences in the macroeconomic system as a whole. In a single visual representation, it captures all five macroeconomic objectives outlined in chapter 1. On the vertical axis, it captures information about the goal of low output price inflation; on the horizontal axis, it captures information about (sustainable) GDP and the long-term objective of GDP growth, as well as about employment and unemployment, which can be interpreted to reflect both labor and capital resources. The back-and-forth movement of the economic system along the horizontal axes captures information about business cycles and whether they are smooth or erratic. Even the need for global economic policy coordination across state jurisdictions is captured, as imports from and exports to other states depend, in part, on economic conditions and policy in those states (see chapter 4). The framework does not, however, address income distribution or development goals (chapter 1).

Postviolence Recovery and Reconstruction

Economies possess an inherent constraint on the supply side, below which the economy's productive capacity is underutilized and above which it is strained. Say that under normal circumstances, an economy is expected to grow, net of output price inflation, by 3 percent per year, its inherent long-term capacity for economic growth. When there is either a demand failure or an input price shock on the supply side so that the economy operates at only 2 percent growth per year, then in the absence of compensatory demand from the public sector, the extra unemployment of labor and capital resources this implies eventually compels workers to accept lower wages (or lower wage increases), increasing profit opportunities and moving supply back to its starting position. Eventually, growth of 3 percent per year is restored. If, in the judgment of authorities, the adjustment process during which unemployed resources lie idle takes too long, government can try to stimulate the economy artificially by increasing government expenditure. In growth, employment, and unemployment, the economy reverts back to its normal long-run inherent capacity, but at the cost of an uptick in output price inflation caused by the artificial stimulation. On the whole, an automatic private sector supply-side correction is preferred over an artificial public sector intervention. In violence-torn economies, however, the private sector is hesitant to invest and understandably waits for the public sector to act first. This creates a two-sided pressure: In periods of slack private economic activity, tax revenues are low while the call for public sector spending is high. Consequently, fiscal deficits and accumulated public sector debt are likely to increase. This is fine so long as borrowing from abroad is possible and not unduly onerous. Whether debt becomes onerous depends, in part, on the conduct of deficit spending—that is, on whether it can bring the private sector fully back into the economy, in which case tax revenue grows and public expenditure needs decline somewhat, so that the debt load can be carried and paid off in time (see below).

Long Run and Short Run

Economists are hard put to define the long-run growth capacity at which to aim an economy. Should policymakers aim at annual economic growth of 2 or 3 percent or at another percentage? In practice, economists tend to use an average growth rate derived from the economy's record of past decades, stipulating that average to be the economy's inherent annual growth limit. For violence-torn countries, especially those emerging from decades of armed conflict, using this yardstick is incorrect. Depending on the remaining capital stock, the growth rebound may at first be very large before settling into a more stable growth pattern. Both the experiences of economic collapse during violence as well as growth afterward can exhibit a wide degree of variation.

Not having a yardstick does not make the idea of having one false, however. Without a target for economic growth, policymakers may be too timid, contenting themselves with, say, 2 percent growth when 3 percent can be achieved safely. Or they may aim at 3 percent growth when the economy's inherent growth limit lies at 2 percent. The danger in either case lies in not knowing what the growth limit is. Both constant overstimulation and too much caution can derail an economy and plunge society back into war.

Fiscal Policy: Governing under Duress

Purpose

Fiscal policy concerns how public sector revenue is raised and spent. It is not a crisis management tool; its primary function is to promote society's orderly development and well-being, that is, its growth and continual betterment. This is usually achieved through a two-pronged approach. One provides enabling environments or conditions that stimulate the private sector. The other provides economic security for population segments that cannot manage on their own. Spending fiscal resources on macroeconomic stabilization, though sometimes necessary, can thus be a costly distraction.[3] This is one reason why, ideally, fiscal policy creates an economic environment that is strong enough to require no stabilization: Just as it is preferable to build rather than strip assets in order to derive income, it is preferable to prevent emergencies rather than to direct resources toward them.

Revenue

Governments can raise funds from many sources. It can tax the income and profits of people and businesses, imports and exports, domestic and tourist spending, and specific products, such as cigarettes. It can also raise revenue by selling natural resource wealth directly, such as realized in petroleum

Fiscal policy concerns how public sector revenue is raised and spent.

export revenues (natural resource rents), or by granting natural resource exploitation licenses to domestic and foreign firms. Governments can charge fees for public services, from driver's license and passport fees to entry fees at national parks, and raise further revenue at the national, provincial, and district or municipal levels. Governments can raise funds by issuing currency (seignorage), by depleting foreign exchange reserves, and by borrowing domestically or abroad, either through private sector financial institutions or from bilateral or multilateral lenders. And governments can receive outright grants, in the forms of development or military aid. Many developing states rely for a major portion of their revenue on natural resource rents. This means that a particular sector of the economy carries a disproportional burden—but often endows it with disproportional political influence as well—while other sectors contribute proportionally less to the public purse. Similarly, public expenditure policy affects particular sectors, such as education, agriculture, or transportation infrastructure, more than others, so that macroeconomic goals are entwined with sectoral and regional goals.

The Tax System

For economists, five criteria characterize a good tax system. First is low costs of administration and compliance, or administrative simplicity. Second is flexibility, a system that can adapt quickly to changing economic and political circumstances. Third is transparency and political accountability. Fourth is fairness across income groups. And fifth is a tax system that can enhance economic efficiency and not distort economic efforts. Excessive income tax rates can lead to tax avoidance (people performing less taxable work) or evasion (not declaring income or moving work to low-tax jurisdictions elsewhere). Perceptions of excessive taxes on capital can lead to inefficiencies in capital markets. By the same token, undertaxing undesirable economic activities, or even subsidizing them, encourages their unabated continuance. Appropriate taxation can mitigate the adverse environmental effects of automobile traffic. Likewise, outright subsidization of certain product categories, such as fuel—or food, for that matter—distorts the economic system. This may be necessary to protect vulnerable populations or maintain the peace, though it may also create powerful vested interests on the supply and the demand sides.

Regarding fairness, the tax system should display horizontal and vertical equity. Horizontal equity means that persons who are equal in every respect should be treated equally in taxation; in tax law, a married couple should not

Horizontal tax equity: a situation in which persons who are equal in every respect should be treated equally in taxation as well. *Vertical tax equity:* a situation in which those capable of paying more do pay more.

be treated differently than an otherwise identical unmarried couple. Vertical equity means that those who can pay more taxes, should pay more. This leaves the political problem of determining income brackets and their tax rates. Some economists argue that because income is the result of a person's contribution to society, it should not be taxed at all. Instead, consumption should be taxed through a sales or value-added tax. This has the beneficial side effect of encouraging saving and providing a pool of loanable funds for investment and future economic growth. This also simplifies the tax system, reduces the administrative cost of tax collection, and limits opportunities for corruption. To protect certain populations from hardship, a state can elect to exempt some consumption categories from taxation, such as food and medications.

Ideal tax specifications do not come about overnight. Especially in violence-afflicted societies, rebuilding a well-functioning tax administration takes years. Some states thus focus revenue-raising efforts on easily taxed areas, such as the export sector, but an unequal burden of taxation induces tax evasion efforts and, with it, carries very real dangers of subverting the state apparatus through corruption. The practical difficulties of rebuilding and then tapping a broad, society-wide tax base should not be underestimated. Dedicated long-term training and capacity rebuilding grants may need to be offered to achieve it.

Debt

Many developing and emerging economies, especially those recovering from violence, find that resource needs far outstrip availability. The resulting budget deficits have led governments to artificially inflate the economy by printing too much money (see below) or to take on unsustainable domestic or external debt burdens. If economic growth generates sufficient revenue to service the debt, it may be sustained indefinitely; governments and companies alike can carry perpetual debt. But unsustainable debt must be lowered. This can be done in three ways: first, by receiving outright debt forgiveness (grants); second, by increasing public revenue and dedicating the extra resources to increase debt service (interest and payoff of debt principals); and third, by decreasing public expenditure and using the saved funds to service the debt. As mentioned above, there is now widespread agreement that public expenditure cuts must detract neither from sensible spending that enhances the framework conditions for growth nor from poverty alleviation. If debt is taken on, it must be focused on uses with the highest long-term social return. The composition of public expenditure may be more important than its level.

Few countries' public sector accounting systems measure annual deficits and accumulated debt properly. The conceptually correct way—for private households, businesses, and governments—is not to focus on revenue minus expenditure streams but on assets minus liabilities, or government net worth. When a debt-financed seaport is built, the liability of the debt is balanced by the asset of the port. The port generates revenues on its own, and by stimulating economic growth, it contributes to higher tax revenue. Thus, the debt incurred can be paid off. In practice, however, most states' budgets include a debt service line item that is not linked to the underlying assets, so it is impossible to assess whether the assets repay their costs. In war-torn states, assets such as seaports frequently suffer loss of business days and physical destruction; the delay in debt repayment or the inability to repay the debt at all should be counted as part of the cost of war.

Using fiscal policy as a tool for macroeconomic stabilization requires that government can issue discretionary spending or forgo tax revenue to leave more spending power in the private sector. This can prop up an economy during recession.[4] In practice, however, developing nations, especially violence-afflicted ones, rarely have discretionary funds or the leisure to forgo tax revenue. The need to draw on funds from global sources is overwhelming. In the past, these have added to unsustainable debt levels, so that in recent years, very low-interest-rate loans, debt relief, debt forgiveness, and outright grants have become more prominent in the fiscal affairs of violence-afflicted states. This suggests a bifurcated approach to fiscal policy, designing, implementing, and adhering to sound fiscal management practice for its own sake and meeting the remaining need from overseas in a nonburdening manner, with the long-term goal—over ten or twenty years' time—of achieving sufficient economic growth from within to gradually crowd out and graduate from overseas assistance.

Public Expenditure Policy and Management

Public expenditure policy aims at overall fiscal discipline, constant reevaluation of spending priorities within the revenue constraint, and operational efficiency. As the World Bank argues,

The interdependence of [these] three levels is one of the most powerful findings of both practice and theory. The pursuit of aggregate fiscal discipline is
often done in such a way as to undermine . . . performance—arbitrarily reor-
dering priorities and devastating service delivery and operational performance more generally. Similarly, a lack of discipline and budgetary realism in
making strategic policy choices leads to a mismatch between policies and
resources, resulting in inadequate funding for operations. More positively,
fiscal stability creates an environment that encourages sound . . . performance. In turn, sound performance . . . feeds back into fiscal stability.[5]

The World Bank lists a range of criteria for budget and financial management that apply to violence-afflicted states as to any other state. First is
comprehensiveness and decision-making discipline, meaning that current
and capital expenditures are properly budgeted. Second is flexibility, avoiding implementation being overly tight and strategy overly loose. Third is
legitimacy, so that those with power to change policy during implementation have participated in policy formulation. Fourth is predictability of the
short-, medium-, and long-term time paths of expenditure flows. Fifth is
contestability, honesty, and information, so that accurate and timely data
can be used in politically and technically unbiased ways to contribute to
expenditure review and evaluation and potential policy changes. Sixth is
transparency for decision-makers and the public and accountability by decision-makers, decision-implementers, and users of public funds.[6]

Foreign Aid

The current consensus regarding aid advises against peak amounts being
delivered immediately after the end of war, when the absorptive capacity
of the postwar state is still limited. Instead, capacity rebuilding needs to be
offered and aid needs to peak perhaps three to five years after the war,
when the institutional capacity to absorb aid has been rebuilt. In a study of
the Democratic Republic of the Congo (DRC), IMF authors write that "we
found that too often international aid to postconflict countries seems to
taper off shortly after a peace agreement is reached, whereas, in fact, appropriate and prolonged aid is needed to consolidate peace and avoid a
reemergence of conflict."[7] Immediate support for social recovery turns out
to be more important and effective than support for reconstruction and
stabilization, as neglecting pressing social priorities can lead to resent-
ment that restarts the violence. Stabilization thus becomes an intermediate aim, and reconstitution and rebuilding of assets a long-term goal. Fiscal

policy and fiscal aid must accommodate this sequencing and balancing. In practice, this involves separate tracks of aid that overlap in timing.

Research by Demekas, McHugh, and Kosma find that "while both humanitarian and reconstruction aid are welfare-enhancing, humanitarian aid reduces long-run capital accumulation and growth. Reconstruction aid, on the other hand, may increase the long-run capital stock and, if carefully designed, avoid the pitfalls of the Dutch disease."[8] This suggests that aid needs to be purposeful and delivered in stages. Reconstruction aid includes aid for intangibles, especially institution building; reestablishment of legal and regulatory systems, judicial and supervisory agencies, and the tax system and administration; and rebuilding of regional trade links. In addition to humanitarian and reconstruction aid, general government budget support aid may be necessary on a continuing basis to rebuild, strengthen, and support ongoing government policy and administrative work. In the IMF's work in the DRC in the early 2000s, it clearly recognized the connection between economics and politics and that aid design—circumstances, objectives, size, time profile, and composition—must account for this connection:

> Three main phases—stabilization, reconstruction, and development—were defined and later included in the country's poverty reduction strategy. The stabilization phase sought to remove the most severe distortions and break the vicious cycle of hyperinflation and declining value of the currency. Priority had to be given to paying the wages of civil servants and the military on time to defuse social tension and rebuild confidence in the public administration. In parallel, with the help of the World Bank, the administrative capacity of key ministries, including the finance ministry and the central bank, had to be buttressed. Replacing lost administrative capacity is a lengthy process because many civil servants were killed during the war. It takes time to train replacements, which underscores the importance of prolonging foreign aid. At the same time, the foundations of a level playing field for the private sector were put in place.[9]

The latter included sequencing of aid to restructure high-impact economic sectors—in the case of the DRC, mining, forestry, and transportation. Thus, how aid is timed, sequenced, and spent is sometimes as important as the issue of creating absorptive capacity per se.

Spillovers

Another finding of recent research—dramatic enough to have led to almost immediate aid policy changes—is that wars can create spillover effects that

FIGURE 3.4. Costa Rica, 1950–2009

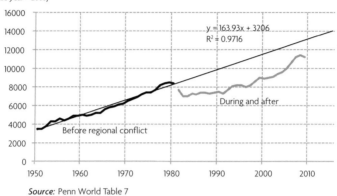

Inflation, population, and purchasing
power parity–adjusted
per capita GDP
(I$, base year = 2005)

$y = 163.93x + 3206$
$R^2 = 0.9716$

During and after

Before regional conflict

Source: Penn World Table 7

adversely affect neighboring states to such a degree that they also need fiscal assistance.[10] Figure 3.4 shows inflation- and purchasing power–adjusted per capita GDP from 1950 to 1980 for Costa Rica, as well as a linear projection to (and beyond) 2009.[11] The actual record for 1981–2009 is also shown. The lost decade of the 1980s—when Costa Rica's neighbors, El Salvador, Guatemala, Honduras, and Nicaragua, all were embroiled in internal wars— starkly manifests itself in the gap between the projected and the actual outcomes. After the peace agreements of the early 1990s, brokered by Costa Rica's then president Oscar Arias, the country's former growth resumed. Still, based on the 1950–80 data, by 2009 per capita production had not reached its projected level. Like its warring neighbors, Costa Rica thus suffered a thirty-year economic penalty even though it was not at war. The cumulative gap between projected and actual per capita GDP between 1981 and 2009 amounts to I$65,062, or about eight times the value of the country's per capita 2009 income—a massive loss.

The knock-on or spillover effects sometimes can be greater in neighboring countries than in the war-torn state. The reasons for this are many, involving the need to deal with possibly millions of refugees, interruption of trade routes and markets, environmental stresses, lost tourist revenue, and higher security expenses in connection with securing border regions and safeguarding refugee encampments. All of these carry fiscal consequences.

Monetary Policy: Dysfunction in a Violent World

Monetary policy deals with the internal and external value of a state's currency—that is, inflation and the currency's foreign exchange value—the determination of interest rates, and the regulation and supervision of a country's banking system. The primary institution is the central bank, and its primary tool consists of influencing the money supply, the amount of money available in the economy to carry out economic transactions. Although the two cannot easily be separated, in this section we deal primarily (but briefly) with some domestic aspects of monetary policy and address (more extensively) foreign exchange–related issues, such as exchange rate mechanisms and regimes, currency valuation, and other matters, in chapter 4.

Monetary Policy Mechanics

To appreciate some of the pitfalls of monetary policy in postwar situations, it helps to first understand the textbook purposes and mechanics of monetary policy. Assume that a commercial bank has made a loan to a private firm. The firm gets the funds and the bank obtains a signed contract, in which the firm promises to repay the loan. This contract, or note, can be sold to the central bank, with the firm now owing the funds

> *Monetary policy* deals with the internal and external (foreign exchange) value of a state's currency, the determination of interest rates, and the regulation and supervision of the banking system.

to the central bank. The central bank can elect to pay the commercial bank for the note by printing money. The commercial bank then can take these new funds and loan them out to yet another customer. By buying notes from commercial banks, a central bank thereby injects additional funds into the economy. Likewise, governments can finance budget deficits by borrowing through domestic financial markets, that is, through commercial and investment banks. The central bank can purchase these notes, again injecting additional funds into the economy. In practice, central banks tend to purchase government-issued debt, not commercial debt, meaning that—perhaps strangely—one arm of government is buying debt issued by another arm, the executive branch. The central bank thus monetizes government debt. The more debt the central bank purchases, the more potential funds are available to commercial banks to loan out. Since commercial banks are for-profit enterprises, a large supply of loanable funds leads them to compete

The *quantity theory of money* argues that overly rapid increases in money supply eventually result in corresponding increases in inflation.

for borrowing customers by lowering the interest rate on loans. So long as the demand for currency (money demand) needed to carry out daily economic transactions is steady, the central bank's injection of money supply leads to lower interest rates and provides an incentive to private households and commercial enterprises to borrow more money. As the point of borrowing is to spend the borrowed funds, an increased money supply spurs economic activity and employment through the aggregate demand side of an economy. If firms borrow funds for financing investment to increase their productivity and expand their businesses, then the supply side of an economy is also affected. The combined effect is that employment and economic growth increase, while inflation is held in check through growth in productivity-enhancing physical investment.

This mechanism, however, requires a deep, well-functioning private financial market and a nearly flawless interface among public policy formulation, policy implementation, and a smooth and easily predictable private sector response. In postwar economies, frequently all three of these are lacking.

The Long and Short Term, Again

Monetary policy may stimulate and support economic growth in the short term, but is no substitute for an independent long-term growth policy. To see this, we introduce—as in chapter 2—an accounting equation, from which one can derive the quantity theory of money, a theory of how the quantity of money in an economy affects other economic variables. The equation is written as (1): $P \times Q = M \times V$, where, on the left-hand side, P stands for the price level in an economy and Q stands for inflation-adjusted, or real, GDP. Together, they amount to an economy's nominal GDP, called Y (see chapter 2). On the right-hand side, M stands for the money supply and V for velocity, or the turnover rate of money. One might think of $M \times V$ as a country's effective money supply, namely, the money supply multiplied by how often each unit of currency is used.

To illustrate, in 2010 the nominal GDP (Y)—the value of goods and services produced—in the United States was USD14,660.2 billion, breaking down into a price level (P) of 1.10654 and real GDP (Q) of 13,248.7.[12] But the amount of money (M)—cash and funds available in checking and saving accounts—to purchase these goods and services was, by one measure, only USD8,629.3 billion. It follows that every dollar must have been used on average 1.69 times, the velocity (V) of money. This makes sense because when a person uses his or her paycheck to purchase groceries, the store deposits the funds and reissues the dollars through paychecks to its employees, who, in turn, make purchases of their own. Thus, every available dollar is used several times over. Cash turns over very often, checking account dollars turn over somewhat less often, and saving account dollars turn over even less often. It turns out that while the turnover rate of money (V) differs from country to country, within a country it tends to be relatively stable from year to year. For practical purposes, V thus may be considered constant, and is then written as V^*.

To make things easier, the following example works with rounded numbers. Let P = 1.1, Q = 14.7, M = 8.6, and V = 1.9. If velocity (V^*) is constant, the first equation can now be rewritten in two informative ways, assuming a second variable also is constant. The first rewriting involves moving the expression Q from the left-hand side to the right-hand side of equation (1). This results in equation (2): $P^* = (M \times V^*) / Q$. In words, the effective money supply divided by a country's real output equals the price level. Now, say we hypothetically change the money supply (M) from USD8.6 trillion to, say, USD9.6 trillion while keeping the price level and the velocity the same. Placing the numbers into equation (2), we obtain $1.1^* = (9.6 \times 1.9^*) / Q$, meaning that the nominal GDP (Q) increases to USD16.6 trillion. In other words, increasing the money supply stimulates the purchase, and hence production, of more goods and services. More production requires labor and capital to work more hours. Earnings increase, and in time, so does overall employment.

But before shopkeepers call manufacturers to increase production, or before manufacturers increase production, shopkeepers might try to raise output prices to deal with the influx of demand. To simulate the extreme case, where all new money shows up only in higher prices, we rewrite the first equation a second time, resulting in equation (3): $Q^* = (M \times V^*) / P$. Once more, we substitute the rounded U.S. numbers to obtain $14.7^* = (9.6 \times 1.9^*) / P$. For the equation to hold, the price level rises from 1.1 to 1.2. In other words, when an economy's supply capacity is constrained, the extra money shows up as output price inflation.

In sum, in the short term, before suppliers notice that there is more money chasing goods, an extra injection of money into the economy can stimulate GDP. But an economy's inherent long-term capacity for growth is limited by its asset base, so that annual GDP growth is constant in the long term, as in equation (3). Thus, an increase of money results in a corresponding increase in the price level. Printing and injecting money into the economy will, over time, not lead to more production but to more inflation. Just as a lubricant alone does not make an engine run, money alone does not make an economy grow.[13] This is why policymakers like to keep money creation under tight control: The consequences of not doing so can be dire. In the long term, it is assets and their productive capacity, not fiscal or monetary policy, that improve peoples' lives. This buttresses once more the need to conduct stabilization policy firmly within the objectives of long-term growth policy.

Dysfunctionalities

The collapse of money and, with it, of monetary policy in violent economies is easily shown by the number of states in which citizens have adopted alternative currencies during and after war. Timor-Leste (East Timor) uses the U.S. dollar as its official currency. So does El Salvador. After 2003, Iraq used euros and dollars before eventually issuing a new dinar. Issuing a new currency after violence is popular: The German reichsmark became the deutschmark after World War II. Both Argentina and Brazil reissued their currencies around the time of their respective military dictatorships and the years thereafter, as both tried to recreate stable, credible currencies and financial markets. Kosovo used the deutschmark before switching (with Germany) to the euro. Montenegro and other follow-on states to the former Yugoslavia also used the euro, regardless of whether or not these states acceded to the European Union. Zimbabweans use a slew of substitute currencies, including the Botswana pula, the British pound, the euro, the U.S. dollar, and the South African rand—anything but the Zimbabwean dollar. The main reason for currency substitution is that war and inflation tend to go together, debasing money's function as a store of value. In Zimbabwe, by the third quarter of 2008, inflation ran at an annual rate of over 500 billion percent.[14] The country's private financial sector collapsed. In essence, a parallel public monetary system, privately managed, emerged. Neither a functioning bank-to-customer nor a functioning bank-to-bank (interbank) market exists. In partially criminalized economies, such as Afghanistan or Colombia, very large sums of money travel through informal channels, circumventing formal private financial institutions and staying outside the reach of public policy influence. Violence undermines the policy assumptions that underlie ordinary monetary purposes and mechanics.

Reconstitution and Coordination

Postwar fiscal policy might require rebuilding the physical and administrative apparatus of state ministries and provincial offices, including capacity building of trained personnel. The institutional rebuilding of monetary policy generally involves a smaller staff and physical facilities. The issues monetary policymakers need to deal with are, however, extremely important and involve, among others, rebuilding the central bank; regaining domestic credibility; reestablishing the internal and external banking and payment systems; rebuilding systems for bank supervision; restarting the provision of credit, especially of access to loans by microbusinesses and small- and medium-sized enterprises (SMEs); reining in the high inflation that ordinarily accompanies periods of violent conflict; and dealing with the consequent currency depreciation on foreign exchange markets. Unlike normally functioning advanced economies, where fiscal and monetary policy are judiciously kept apart to provide for independent policy judgment and implementation, in postwar emerging and developing economies, monetary and fiscal policy should be closely coordinated, following politically set objectives of employment and growth, and transitioning only later to independent roles. Monetary policy might initially be more forgiving in its goal of reducing inflation so as to support employment and growth objectives and aim at a phased-in reduction of inflation over an agreed-upon, but credible, time frame.[15]

Institutions and Policies

In addition to domestic institutions, the WBG and IMF have roles to play in forming fiscal and monetary policy. Following the first worldwide oil-price shock in 1973–74, many developing and emerging economies suffered from drastic internal economic mismanagement and a difficult foreign trade, debt, and exchange rate environment. The IMF provides short-term balance of payment–related financial assistance on the condition that economic policy in the recipient state change in particular ways. This conditionality—required, in part, to ensure that states can repay funds borrowed from other member states—has been subject to much criticism. In brief, from the mid-1970s to the mid-1980s, the IMF loaned funds on concessional terms to particularly needy low-income member states. This was handled through a lending facility known as the Trust Fund, replaced in March 1986 by a Structural Adjustment Facility (SAF), followed by an Enhanced Structural

Adjustment Facility (ESAF) in December 1987. In September 1996, the ESAF was made a permanent lending instrument, and replaced in November 1999 by the IMF's Poverty Reduction and Growth Facility (PRGF).

Short-term macroeconomic stabilization can be, and frequently has been, associated with great economic pain. In the past, structural adjustment programs (SAPs) have been carried out through central government budget cuts and the raising of tax or other revenue, with the aim of reducing government budget deficits. This reduces the need for unsustainable borrowing or inflationary money printing. The programs have included demands to properly value the local currency on the foreign exchange market and to improve macroeconomic policies so that private investors feel confident to once again sink money into a country. The view that these measures can reduce economic growth and increase economic dislocation, unemployment, and poverty may be simultaneously correct in the short term and incorrect in the medium term, over which the IMF tends to evaluate success or failure. In the 2011 financial and political crisis in Greece, in exchange for the actual release of an already approved tranche of financial aid, eurozone countries and the IMF demanded substantial budgetary changes from the Greek government which, in turn, had to be pushed through the Greek parliament and ultimately be endorsed by that country's population. As elsewhere, this is inducing fights over the redistribution of future income or other tax obligations, or cuts in benefits or services where those who are poor or politically voiceless may be expected to bear the larger share of the burden.

The IMF has refuted wholesale, undifferentiated criticism, but has acknowledged the adverse effects of its mandated policies. By the late 1990s, one consequence of this acknowledgment was that the IMF asked governments to leave social expenditure on education and health care untouched, or even to increase it. In some cases, this clause was written into the conditionality agreement. Even so, in many cases the poor still suffered, and the IMF then agreed to work more closely with the World Bank and civil society to better protect particularly vulnerable populations; hence the introduction of the PRGF.

The PRGF was replaced in 2009 by a Poverty Reduction and Growth Trust (PRGT) with three loan facilities. The Extended Credit Facility (ECF) is the direct successor to the PRGF in the sense of providing "financial assistance to countries with protracted balance of payments problems" but with the important qualification that "ECF-supported programs should be based on the country's own development strategy and aim to safeguard social objectives."[16]

Thus, IMF programs have gone through three stages of development, from imposing conditions on poor states that had little choice but to accept them, to softer conditions that reflected World Bank and civil society concerns especially in regard to poverty reduction, to, today, conditions that are being led by the affected low-income countries' own views on poverty reduction and growth. In this, the IMF emphasizes widespread public participation and ownership of poverty reduction strategies in the affected states. It is flexible about how states achieve poverty reduction and growth objectives so long as macroeconomic stability is not threatened. It also highlights good governance in terms of public resource management, transparency, and accountability.

FAILURE AND SUCCESS: Two Case Studies

FAILURE AND CONTRAST: ZIMBABWE AND BOTSWANA

Figure 3.5 compares inflation- and purchasing power–adjusted per capita GDP, as well as the per capita personal consumption levels out of GDP, of Botswana and Zimbabwe. Botswana became an independent state in 1966. In the same year, the Rhodesian civil war of liberation from white rule began in Zimbabwe. This lasted until 1979, and Zimbabwe attained independence in 1980. Except for rough patches in the early to mid-1990s when South Africa abandoned apartheid and the shock of the 2009 world financial crisis, Figure 3.5 shows Botswana's economic output per person growing fifteenfold, from I$578 in 1960 to I$8,872 in 2009. Consumption grew more moderately, about eightfold, from I$492 to I$4,126.

In the years following Zimbabwe's independence in 1980, President Robert Mugabe gradually repressed white and rival black opponents alike, engaged in murderous campaigns, and got involved in the DRC's bloody war (1998–2002). Zimbabwe's economic output per person—lower than Botswana's to begin with—fell by almost half, from I$280 in 1960 to I$143 in 2009, as did consumption. The country saw negative economic growth in seven of the past ten years. By late 2008, inflation was said to be running at over 500 quintillion percent—a one followed by eighteen zeroes. In January 2009 the central bank introduced a Z$100 trillion banknote.

The prevalence of HIV/AIDS in Zimbabwe is high; average life expectancy has plummeted across the region, and both Botswana's and Zimbabwe's figures are now under forty years of age, although Botswana's life expectancy at birth is nearing sixty years of age again. But Zimbabweans

FIGURE 3.5. Botswana (1960–2009) and Zimbabwe (1954–2009)

Inflation, population, and purchasing power
parity–adjusted per capita GDP and consumption
(I$, base year = 2005)

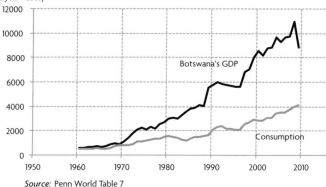

Source: Penn World Table 7

Inflation, population, and purchasing power
parity–adjusted per capita GDP and consumption
(I$, base year = 2005)

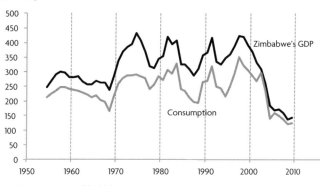

Source: Penn World Table 7

also have fled their country in droves. White farmers, who once made Zimbabwe the breadbasket of the region, were driven out a few years ago. Blacks have followed by the tens of thousands, often going to Botswana.

Botswana's economy in based on minerals—diamonds, copper, nickel, and platinum. Exports account for half of GDP (nondiamond exports for 20 percentage points, diamonds for 30 percentage points), though nonmineral GDP growth is higher than that of mineral-based GDP growth, indicating that the economy is diversifying. Inflation, in the 5 to 10 percent range over the past few years, is relatively modest. The government's fiscal position and the banking system are considered sound. Private investment in the economy is high, as are the country's foreign exchange reserves to cover import needs. The World Bank considers Botswana an upper-middle-income country, even if unemployment and poverty rates are high, as is inequality of income distribution.

In contrast, Zimbabwe is an utterly collapsed state. Virtually no one does business in Zimbabwean dollars anymore. The economy, or what is left of it, is run with substitute currencies, especially the South African rand and U.S. dollar. For all practical purposes, private banking has ceased, government debt is extraordinarily high, and foreign exchange reserves are near zero. There is no functioning protection of private property rights, the rule of law is absent, and no one invests in the country. Two-thirds of its people are in poverty, nearly half the population is undernourished, and infant mortality is rising, as is maternal mortality upon giving birth. Total government revenue collapsed from USD942 million in 2005 to an estimated USD133 million in 2008, about what some Wall Street bankers still made in that year.

The reasons for the difference in economic performance are easy to discern. Zimbabwe does not have a functioning political system; Botswana does. Even if, as until recently in Japan, one party tends to win all the national campaigns, Botswana's elections nonetheless are freely and nonviolently contested. When they come, the post-Mugabe years in Zimbabwe could be disastrous. But perhaps the example of Botswana will inspire imitation. After all, Zimbabwe is equally well endowed with natural resource wealth.

SUCCESS: CHILE

From 1973 to 1990, Chile went through a period of military dictatorship. As may be seen in figure 3.6, per capita GDP, adjusted for inflation and measured in international dollars (I\$), grew throughout the 1950s and 1960s, stalled in the early 1970s, and plummeted during the early years of the Pinochet dictatorship. A period of renewed growth was followed by another collapse in the early 1980s. During the Pinochet years consumption never exceeded the high point of Allende's last year, 1972. Post-Pinochet, a period of sustained, rapid growth ensued that, by now, has led Chile to be the most well-off country in South America. It is the subcontinent's only member of the Organisation for Economic Co-operation and Development (OECD).

FIGURE 3.6. Chile, 1960–2009

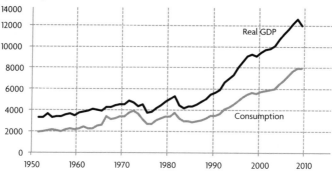

Inflation, population, and purchasing
power parity–adjusted
per capita GDP and consumption
(I$, base year = 2005)

Source: Penn World Table 7

Chile follows sound and consistent fiscal and monetary policies, with transparency, predictability, and credibility. In some regards, Chile is a world leader in economic policy innovation. Begun during the dictatorship, its policies have been continued through several democratically elected administrations. With few exceptions, state enterprises have been privatized, by far the largest exception being Codelco, the copper mining giant. The retirement or pension plan fund has been privatized and international trade has been fostered through numerous free trade agreements. Chile has seen recurrent government budget surpluses that permitted the country to respond to the 2008–09 world economic crisis, which had badly affected its export-dependent economy, with a domestic stimulus program that will not unduly burden the country's medium-term position. Since 2001 Chile has adhered to an explicit structural fiscal rule, codified into law in 2006, that requires the government to run a small annual budget surplus over the business cycle. In this way, surpluses are accumulated during times of an expanding economy, to be used to prop up falling domestic demand during contraction, as in 2009.

FDI is high, albeit focused on the extractive and utilities fields and often in the form of acquisitions of existing assets rather than the financing of new capital formation. Despite continuous, rapid growth, population-wide educational achievements are lacking, and income inequality and poverty rates still are high. The country needs to manage a transition to a more broad-based and inclusive social and economic policy framework.

In monetary policy, the central bank is independent, the currency floats freely on the world market, and interest policy is handled flexibly in light of economy-wide needs. There are no restrictions on foreign investors bringing funds in or repatriating profits. Consumer inflation is targeted at around 3 percent and generally held there (apart from exceptional periods, such as the 2008–09 crisis). All in all, Chile has made good policy choices, combined with consistent implementation.

Policy Lessons and Tips

LESSON 3.1: Short-term needs should be met, but with consideration for their effects in the long term.

LESSON 3.2: The AD/AS framework allows at least the provisional analysis of many proximate causes and consequences of changes in aggregate demand, aggregate supply, and economic policy.

LESSON 3.3: Everyone agrees on the worthiness of securing a stable macroeconomic environment. The disagreements are over the detail, mechanics, sequencing, magnitude, and length of aid, not over the goal itself.

LESSON 3.4: The purpose of fiscal and monetary policy is not crisis management. It is better to prevent macroeconomic instability than to use costly fiscal and monetary resources for stabilization. Economically inappropriate macroeconomic policy can be as damaging as war.

LESSON 3.5: A good tax system is simple, flexible, transparent, fair, and economically efficient. A good expenditure system is disciplined, operationally efficient, and routinely reevaluates spending priorities within the revenue constraint.

LESSON 3.6: Postwar aid should be offered over the long term (up to ten years), not short term (one or two years).

LESSON 3.7: The ultimate aim must be the reconstitution of assets. The intermediate aim must be macroeconomic stabilization. The immediate aim must be to assist hurting populations. Policy must accommodate this sequencing, overlapping, and balancing of aid. Neighbors of war-afflicted countries also need help.

LESSON 3.8: Money accommodates economic growth; it does not make an economy grow by itself.

LESSON 3.9: Violence can create dysfunctionalities regarding the formulation and conduct of fiscal and monetary policy. If unaddressed, it is unlikely that war-torn societies can be rebuilt into functioning entities.

LESSON 3.10: Not all violence-afflicted states are completely atypical. In seeking and providing policy advice and technical support, all sides should be pragmatic, not dogmatic.

Notes

1. UNDP, *Post-Conflict Economic Recovery*, xxiii.
2. The usual textbook presentation is not in terms of percentages on the horizontal and vertical axes, but levels of GDP and output prices. However, a change from one to another level of GDP can be expressed as a percentage change, as can changes in average prices. Thus, although our graph is incorrect in the strict textbook sense, for the purposes that interest us, little harm is done relative to the benefit of a clearer exposition of the issues at hand.
3. For example, the many hundreds of billions of dollars governments spent to rein in the world economic crisis of 2009 amount to tax obligations for future taxpayers. Early recognition, intervention, and prevention would have been cheaper for taxpayers and the affected populations.
4. Alternately, government can raise tax rates or cut spending to throttle the economy when it is growing too fast, but a fast-growing economy, so long as output price inflation is kept in check and does not ignite social inequities, can hardly be viewed as a problem.
5. World Bank, *Public Expenditure Management Handbook* (Washington, DC: World Bank, 1998), 3, http://siteresources.worldbank.org/INTPEAM/Resources/pem98.pdf.
6. See World Bank, *Public Expenditure.*
7. IMF, "Democratic Republic of the Congo: Lessons from the Ashes of Conflict," *IMF Survey* 34, no. 4 (March 2005), 61.
8. D.G. Demekas, J. McHugh, and T. Kosma, "The Economics of Post Conflict Aid," IMF working paper no. WP/02/198, International Monetary Fund, Washington, DC, 2002, 1. Dutch disease refers to the influx of large amounts of foreign aid that can lead to the appreciation of the local currency and make the aid recipient country's exports noncompetitively expensive on foreign markets.
9. "Democratic Republic of the Congo," 61–62.

10. See, e.g., J. Murdoch and T. Sandler, "Civil Wars and Economic Growth: A Regional Comparison," *Defence and Peace Economics,* 13, no. 6 (2002), 451–64; I. Saleyhan and K.S. Gleditsch, "Refugees and the Spread of Civil War," *International Organization,* 60 (2006), 335–66; and literature cited there.

11. Statistically speaking, an upward-bending exponential function or a polynominal function of order 2 both fit the data slightly better, but upon visual inspection would evidently overfit the data.

12. A price level of 1.10654 means 10.654 percent higher prices in 2010 than in the base year (2005).

13. There is one other option: (4) $M^* = (P \times Q) / V^*$. Here, money and velocity are assumed unchanged (M^*; V^*). An increase in prices must come at the expense of a decrease in production, or vice versa.

14. International Monetary Fund, "Zimbabwe," *Country Report* no. 09/139, Washington, DC, 2009.

15. G. del Castillo, *Rebuilding War-Torn States: The Challenge of Post-Conflict Economic Reconstruction* (Oxford: Oxford University Press, 2008), 281; UNDP, *Post-Conflict Economic Recovery,* xxiii.

16. See International Monetary Fund, "IMF Extended Credit Facility," factsheet, http://www.imf.org/external/np/exr/facts/ecf.htm.

4

THE GLOBAL ECONOMY
International Trade and Finance

This chapter deals with how countries and international actors can monitor and manage their trade and associated financial flows. War and violence upset this management, as there is little that even a well-intentioned government of a violence-afflicted state can do about the mechanics of international trade and finance. Moreover, mismanagement of trade and finance can itself be a cause of conflict. Understanding the mechanics—beginning with the balance of payments—is key to avoiding situations that can lead to instability and, sometimes, war.

The Balance of Payments

Ordinarily divided into two parts—the current account and the financial and capital account—the balance of payments (BoP) is an accounting frame-

> The *balance of payments* is an accounting framework that tracks the monetary value of a country's imports and exports of goods and services as well as the corresponding financial flows. The frameworks consists of credits (inflows) and debits (outflows), which must sum to zero; by definition, the balance of payments must actually balance.

TABLE 4.1 Balance of Payments, El Salvador, 2005 (US$ millions)

Item	Credit/Exports US$ Inflow (+) US$ Demand	Debit/Imports US$ Outflow (–) US$ Supply	Balance
1. Current account			–893
1.1 Merchandise	+3,429	–6,534	
1.2 Services (net)		–82	
1.3 Income (net)		–571	
1.4 Unilateral transfers (net)	+2,865		
2. Financial and capital account			+947
2.1 Capital transfers (net)	+94		
2.2 Public sector (net)	+329		
2.3 Private sector (net)	+470		
2.4 Change in net reserves (– = increase)	+59		
2.5 Other		-5	
3. Statistical discrepancy		-54	-54
4. Balance (should be zero)	+7,246	-7,246	0

Source: "El Salvador," Country Report no. 08/101, Washington, DC, IMF, 2009

work that countries use to track the monetary value of the import and export of goods and services as well as the corresponding financial flows. In
essence, the BoP is a giant checkbook, recording debit and credit entries for
outgoing and incoming payments. As an example, table 4.1 reports BoP data
for El Salvador for 2005. All monetary entries are in terms of its currency,
but because El Salvador has adopted the U.S. dollar as its own currency, its
BoP entries are in U.S. dollars.

The merchandise entry in line 1.1 in table 4.1 records the dollar value of
the inflow and outflow of tangible goods into and out of El Salvador. When
exports leave the country, corresponding payments flow into the country.
Foreign purchasers of goods first demand dollars on the foreign exchange
market. The dollars thus acquired then flow into El Salvador. This is treated
as a checkbook credit item; hence the plus sign. Conversely, when El Salvador imports, say, machine tools from Germany, dollars flow out of El Salvador to the foreign exchange markets to be converted into euros to pay the
suppliers. The BoP treats this as a debit entry, with a minus sign (dollar
outflow) attached. As table 4.1 shows, for 2005 there was a USD3 billion net
outflow related to merchandise trade (USD3,429 million minus USD6,534 =
–USD3,114 million, or –USD3.1 billion).

Services—that is, trade in intangible items—are recorded in line 1.2. For example, the dollar value of insurance and transportation services Salvadoran households and firms bought abroad is recorded here. The line item also records services for tourists, who bring in dollars. In 2005 the net effect of service trade amounted to an outflow of USD82 million (negative sign in the BoP). Firms and people in El Salvador also make short-term overseas loans (of less than one year of maturity) and take up such loans. Interest received (+ sign) or paid (– sign) is recorded as income (line 1.3). For 2005 the net effect was –USD571 million. The positive and negative entries for unilateral transfers also are netted out already. These resulted in a net inflow of dollars of USD2.865 billion in 2005 (about 17 percent of GDP that year), mostly from Salvadorans who worked abroad and sent money back home to their families. Since the transactions were one-sided—that is, taking place without a direct countertransaction—the term *unilateral transfer* is used.

When all the pluses and minuses in the current account are summed up, the net result for 2005 is an outflow of dollars of USD893 million—the first item in the last numerical column of the table—or about USD3.4 million per working day. Foreign recipients must recycle this overhang of dollars in some way. Some quantity of dollars is used for the illegal trade—of narcotics, for example—and dollars are also employed to conduct trade in the world energy markets. For the German producer selling machine tools to El Salvador, however, there really are only two options. The first is to keep the dollars and invest them in El Salvador, say, to build up a local distribution network, so that the outflow and inflow of dollars cancel each other out. The second option is to sell the earned dollars (for euros) to whoever wants to buy them. Potential buyers include commercial and central banks. Ownership of the dollars would be transferred from one party to another. But it does not make much sense for a commercial or a central bank to buy dollars and hold them. The purpose is to invest them, and the only sensible place to invest them is in or through the financial markets, where the funds come from and where they can earn interest. In the end, the money the machine tool producer earns flows back to El Salvador, albeit with a change in ownership. (For the case of a dollarized

---

The *current account* reflects the monetary value of a country's international trade in goods and services. The *financial and capital account* records nontrade flows. Excepting a *statistical discrepancy*, the two accounts balance out.

economy like El Salvador's, the dollars can likewise flow into the United States or other dollar-using countries. We abstract from that possibility here.)[1] The financial and capital account records the net flowback of dollars through private and official channels. In 2005 this amounted to USD947 million. Relative to the current account, the statistical discrepancy in line 3 is USD54 million—often called errors and omissions—so that in line 4 all the various positive and negative values sum to zero. Porous borders and cash transactions mean that BoP accounting cannot capture all economic activity, so that even if the statistical discrepancy were zero, probably there would still be unaccounted-for activity, for example due to illegal narcotics trade.

By definition, the BoP must always sum to zero. In spite of media and political usage to the contrary, there is no such thing as a BoP surplus or deficit. There can be a current account surplus or deficit, which must be balanced by corresponding, canceling flows in the financial and capital account. Economists are not worried about the existence of a statistical discrepancy so long as it is sometimes positive and sometimes negative over the years (suggesting random fluctuations) and small relative to the sum total of currency inflows and outflows. For El Salvador in 2005 the sum of inflows and outflows amounted to about USD14.5 billion, so that the error of USD54 million is indeed small.

As to some of the specific items in the finance and capital account (line 2), the public sector entry largely reflects foreign aid inflows (grants), while the private sector entry reflects inflows of dollars when foreign companies buy up companies in El Salvador (e.g., in the commercial banking sector). The change in net reserves refers to foreign exchange holdings of the central bank. When it sells dollars to acquire, say, euros, dollars flow out (a minus sign), but the central bank's holdings of euros increase. Thus—counterintuitive but logical within the BoP framework—an increase in holdings of foreign currency takes a minus sign in the BoP. Conversely, a decrease in foreign currency holdings takes a plus sign, as occurred in 2005.

The effects of war, crime, and other forms of violence can show up in the BoP in a variety of ways, such as reduced tourism income (inflows) or more arms purchases (outflows). The importance of remittances and foreign aid, both important consequences of El Salvador's 1979–91 civil war, was already hinted at. We take up some of the violence-related issues pertaining to trade and finance as reflected in the BoP in the next two sections.

The Benefits of Trade

No one doubts the importance of trade within countries. Crossing jurisdictional borders when trade takes place between New York and California in the United States ordinarily raises no problem at all. By analogy, the political borders between the United States and Canada and between the United States and Mexico should raise no problems either. So long as trade is voluntary, it is mutually beneficial, even if the net benefits of trade may not be shared equally between trading parties. There almost always are fierce political fights over the distribution of the wealth that trade creates, but from the bazaars of Asia to the village markets of Africa and the roadside stalls of Latin America, people intuitively understand the benefits of trade.

To enhance their own productivity, people use their labor power to specialize in only one or at most a few economic activities in which they produce a surplus, to be traded against the surpluses that others produce. Today, virtually no one is entirely self-sufficient. Incessant, extensive, and dense trade is a universal necessity, both for those who have attained a modern, high standard of living as well as for those who aspire to it. What irks is not the presence of trade but its absence or manipulation to tweak the net benefits more to one side than the other.

Determinants of Trade

Before political state borders existed—modern-day European borders were made firm not even 150 years ago and, with the development of the European Union, are already breaking down again—the borders that mattered were primarily geographic, and what mattered about them were benefits and costs, such as production, communication, and transportation costs. Geography bestows advantages and disadvantages in the distribution of natural resources, land, soil, freshwater, and sea access. It is unwise to try to produce tropical fruit north of the Arctic Circle or grow lettuce in the Sahel. In addition, geography helps determine transportation costs. It is no surprise that immediate neighbors trade at higher volumes with each other than they do with more distant partners, especially where distance includes considerations of topography. The phenomenon of globalization, meanwhile, always has been partly about spatial reach—the ability to overcome geographic distance through technology—though emerging and developing economies still rely on trade in raw materials and agricultural products, as well as on remittances from migrant workers (e.g., Filipino nurses, Bangladeshi oil field workers, Mexican farmhands).

To facilitate internal and external trade, violence-afflicted states need to rebuild and develop their infrastructure capacity after conflict, especially roads, seaports, and airports, and revamp their institutional capacity to knowledgeably, effectively, and efficiently reintegrate into the world trading system and deal with a host of issues, including terms of trade, tariffs and customs, special economic zones, and overdependence on sectors such as mining. In this regard, statistics from the World Trade Organization (WTO) reveal two important facts. One is that international merchandise trade is dominated by neighborhood effects (intraregional trade) and this, in turn, is highly correlated to transport infrastructure. The other is that world trade in manufactured items has grown much faster than trade in fuels and mining products, which, in turn, have grown slightly faster than trade in agricultural products.[2] Both of these facts bode ill for landlocked, war-torn states with little infrastructure and poorly skilled populations. Transportation services, especially tourism, have also grown hugely. Tourism is one of the largest industries in the world, but for obvious reasons, dangerous locations attract very little of it even if the infrastructure is in place to host overseas visitors. Transportation and safety go together; it is probably no accident that terrorists strike tourist-related targets so frequently. Similarly, unexploded remnants of war—uncleared land and naval mines, improvised explosive devices—can lead to land and sea routes being excluded from economic service for a long time. Angola and Cambodia still suffer from this, as do Chechnya and Nagorno-Karabakh, among the most heavily mined regions in the world. In the latter two, as in Sri Lanka, rebel forces appear to have placed mines as a fence to secure and hold territory, creating numerous postwar problems. From an operational point of view, this suggests that peace negotiations should include talks and agreements regarding the postwar reconstruction of infrastructure for internal and external trade.

The Natural Resource Curse?

In a 2008 report, the African Development Bank (AfDB) distinguished between risk factors that may predispose a community or state to experience large-scale violence and triggers that may release latent violence. The risk factors are the presence of natural resources; low income; low economic growth; ethnic antagonisms; neighborhood effects and external instigation of armed conflict; geography and large populations; a youth bulge, especially proportionally large numbers of young men between fifteen and twenty-nine years of age; political repression and corruption; competition for scarce resources; inequality; religious extremism; a flawed or incomplete transition to democracy; high military expenditure and large armies; diasporas; colonialism and superpower rivalries; and the existence of previous conflicts.[3] Triggers include the attainment of political independence or statehood, regime change, and military coups; elections; neighboring conflicts; and other dramatic events. None of these guarantee the outbreak of violence: Botswana is blessed with natural resource wealth without experiencing large-scale violence, despite achieving statehood, holding contested elections, and having large neighbors prone to violence. The risk factors and triggers are extracted from comparative, cross-country statistical work, but with the firm understanding that the local historical context and the quality of policy- and decision-making matter.[4]

Nonetheless, in specific cases, the availability of natural resources has encouraged capture, especially when—for example, with the end of the Cold War—external financing for contesting parties dried up. The relevant dynamic is simple: Wars cannot be fought without money. Thus, when external financing fails (e.g., state sponsorship, diaspora financing), internal sources are needed. This includes illegal harvesting of tropical timbers, diamond and other mining, or illicitly raising and selling crops with narcotic properties. In traditional state-on-state war, armed violence disrupted trade;[5] in the post–Cold War era, consumers in advanced economies share responsibility for violence that takes place elsewhere insofar as the financing of organized crime and collective violence depends on global distribution and consumption networks and trade opportunities.[6] Global NGO efforts to create voluntary regulatory frameworks, most famously Global Witness's work to impede trade in conflict goods through the Kimberley Process Certification Scheme (KPCS), are themselves liable to be taken hostage by vested interests. KPCS evolved into a producer and distributor cartel in which violence-prone states such as India, Indonesia, Israel, and Zimbabwe were and are members in good standing, while a reformed, post–Charles Taylor Liberia for many years was not. (For related reasons, Global Witness withdrew from the KPCS in December 2011.)[7]

Trade Impediments

Establishing or reestablishing welfare-enhancing legitimate trade is important. Constructing, reconstructing, and upgrading trade-related physical infrastructure, streamlining border and customs procedures, reducing or eliminating import and export taxes, and pursuing trade opportunities especially with immediate neighbors are crucial for economic growth within and across political jurisdictions. But global trade is biased against economically developing states. As mentioned above, compared to ODA of about USD100 billion in 2006,[8] global workers' remittances of USD300 billion in 2006[9] and FDI of over USD1 trillion[10] are very large. Truly opening global markets probably would have an even larger effect. The dollar values of trade distortion policies are extremely complex to compute, but agricultural producer support estimates (PSEs) amounted, for example, to USD280 billion in 2004 for the OECD countries—three times the value of ODA—and estimates for the average annual level of U.S. agricultural subsidies between 1995 and 2001 run between USD14 billion and USD66 billion. EU-15 agricultural subsidies run into the tens of billions of euros.[11] If these were eliminated, the benefits would accrue to developing states, postwar states among them. In short, the value of trade impediments is much higher than the value of aid made available to postconflict states. The blame for the substantial risk of war renewal[12] because of a lack of economic growth thus lies in part with the protectionist policies of economically advanced economies, an issue that has arisen in relations between the European Union and the North African and Middle Eastern (MENA) countries in the wake of the 2011 uprisings. As peace negotiations among conflicting parties in emerging and developing states frequently involve participation by advanced economies, raising the issue of negotiating unrestrained access to global markets may be helpful.

Violence and International Finance

This section describes some of the mechanisms of international finance before moving on to describe and discuss dysfunctions and problems related to violence-afflicted states.

Exchange Rates

Like food and drink, household goods, and other ordinary items, most currencies can be bought and sold on markets. The main economic purpose of

Under *currency appreciation,* one unit of home currency can buy a larger amount of foreign currency than before. The home currency is said to have become stronger. An appreciating currency eases imports but hinders exports as foreign products become relatively cheaper to home customers and home products relatively more expensive to foreign customers.

trading currency is to facilitate the exchange of trade and services across currency boundaries. When a French tourist in South Africa supplies euros in exchange for rand, the supply of euros (EUR) increases, as does the demand for rand (ZAR). If the original exchange rate was ZAR12/EUR1, then the extra supply of euros drives down its price so that its value drops. Now South Africans have to pay, say, only ten rand per euro (ZAR10/EUR1), and Europeans have to pay more euros per rand. From South Africa's view, the consequence of the French tourist is that European goods become cheaper: One euro worth of European products now costs South Africa only ten rand instead of twelve. The euro's currency depreciation is matched by the rand's corresponding currency appreciation: South African products become more expensive for Europeans, so that South African firms have a harder time selling products for export. The tourism sector's gain comes at the expense of all other export sectors.

Returning to the macroeconomic framework introduced in chapter 3, an appreciating currency is expected to diminish trade exports (X) and encourage trade imports (M), so that the net effect of (X – M) should result in a smaller trade surplus (or a larger trade deficit), which, in turn, leads to declining aggregate demand and reduces economic growth and employment—though tourism stimulates the local economy through demand for local accommodation, food, transportation, and so on. Currency appreciation or depreciation therefore amounts to a restructuring of the domestic economy, or, at a minimum, generates pressure to restructure. It involves tradeoffs among economic sectors that stand to gain or to lose from currency fluctuations. Restructuring does not proceed smoothly and creates its own conflicts. Exchange rate depreciation may run into a constraint of insufficient transport infrastructure to make use of sudden external trade opportunities. Conversely, expensive infrastructure may sit idle in fast exchange appreciation.

Most countries favor a strong or high-value, appreciating currency, for at least two reasons. First, cheaper imports benefit the consumers and importers of intermediate goods needed for the production of goods and services. Together, these tend to put a lid on consumer and producer price inflation and leave consumers with extra money to spend on additional consumption (or saving). That said, cheaper imports can threaten domestic producers, and hence employment markets, and are thus unwelcome at a large scale. The second reason why a high-value currency can be desirable is that it compels domestic producers to become more efficient to defend (or regain) their domestic market despite import threats. A government that artificially cheapens its currency in effect subsidizes local producers, giving them the message that production efficiencies are not desired, or that inefficiencies will be tolerated. To deal with short-term exigencies, this may be acceptable politically (and even economically), but not as a long- or even medium-term strategy. Economic growth depends on growing net investment and productivity. Undermining this process is self-defeating.

Exchange Rate Regimes

The currency appreciation and depreciation mechanism requires that two currency regions maintain a flexible exchange rate regime toward each other, whereby their currencies' values are determined primarily by the market rather than by monetary authorities. These authorities—the central bank, but sometimes the ministry of finance or another government agency—can sell or buy currencies and thus influence the market, but they tend to do this only to offset unusually large movements in currency values. Currency market intervention can also be done on a routine basis—called a managed float—to move a particular currency from one exchange rate position to another more smoothly than the private market might do. In the extreme, governments buy or sell their own currency regularly enough to create a fixed exchange rate regime, holding the currency's value at least within a narrow, desired band.[13] This is an implicit price control, and despite notable exceptions—Denmark and Venezuela—it is primarily used by fairly small island economies.

The popular press sometimes gives the impression that flexible exchange rates are good and fixed exchange rates are bad. This can be true, but so can the opposite: A flexible exchange rate regime can promote instability, just as a fixed exchange rate regime can fulfill macroeconomic stabilization functions. Much depends on a country's specific circumstances. If the government of a

A *flexible exchange rate regime* means that a country's monetary authorities normally do not intervene in the private markets that determine the value of the country's currency.

war-torn or postwar state—or any state, for that matter—pegs its currency to the euro or another widely traded, stable currency, as have Kosovo, Timor-Leste, and El Salvador, it hands monetary policy to the country whose currency it adopts. Thus, if a large amount of euro-denominated aid is made available, it would be exchanged at a fixed rate and spent domestically. To adopt a foreign currency as one's own or to stipulate a fixed exchange rate then amounts to the same thing: For all practical purposes, a currency union is created. The domestic currency cannot appreciate, and either undermines export prospects or artificially cheapens imports. A credible fixed exchange rate policy guarantees foreign investors that private monies put into the country can be extracted again at an a priori known rate. Nonetheless, exchange rates that fail to keep pace with the changing conditions of the underlying economies can become a source of macroeconomic instability. After World War II the world's major economies agreed on a system of fixed exchange rates. It was successful for the period of postwar reconstruction, but collapsed spectacularly in 1971. Europe and Japan had recovered from the war and rebuilt their economies. As their productivity improved—and as productivity improved at different rates within Europe—more competitive product pricing on the world market became possible. Adherence to a fixed exchange rate system under these conditions became unduly burdensome. It was like saying that an hour's worth of work must always be exchanged for the same hourly compensation, regardless of the worker's productivity.

Colonial-Era Currency Unions

The currencies of twelve states of the former French colonial empire in Central and West Africa still are tied to France through the Central African CFA franc and the West African CFA franc, denoted XAF and XOF, respectively. Formerly fixed to the French franc, they now are fixed to the euro.[14] Created in 1945, the CFA was devalued repeatedly, either relative to the French franc or with the French franc against other currencies. But on the whole the CFA value was so high as to subsidize—that is, artificially cheapen—European imports for African urban elites and to penalize agroexport-dependent farmers, who lost market share, employment, and income opportunities when foreign customers switched to have their needs supplied from farmers elsewhere in the world. Cacao producers in Côte d'Ivoire or Cameroon cannot effectively compete with Ghana or Nigeria (or Brazil or Indonesia, to round out the list of the world's top six producers) when their exchange rates cannot adjust. The CFA countries could produce and sell more cacao, but an artificially high CFA value induces importers to purchase from non-CFA countries. Thus, production structures are distorted all around the world.[15] The connection to lack of employment and economic growth—and therefore to the lack of peace—becomes evident.

Foreign Capital Flows

A flexible exchange rate regime implies that large amounts of foreign aid—including wages and salaries of aid workers—and remittances of migrants' overseas earnings increase the demand for the local currency, leading to its appreciation. This makes it more difficult for a violence-afflicted state to export products and earn the foreign exchange required to purchase needed imports, even as it becomes cheaper to import products that compete with local production and, hence, local employment and economic growth. The consequent slack in domestic aggregate demand reduces price pressures and tends to hold inflation down—an important and welcome side effect. But as the primary need is to rebuild productive economic activity, governments often resort to debt-financed government projects. The combined effect can be the crowding out of private by publicly financed economic activity, large government budget deficits, and BoP difficulties. Fear of this unsustainable economic strategy was the reason for the IMF's harsh policies: Bringing government finances under control through spending cuts was deemed necessary, even if it damaged production, employment, and growth. The IMF's painful type of structural adjustment can encourage eventual FDI, but if it takes too long to arrive, the social pain can lead to resumption of violent conflict. Moreover, in the immediate postconflict period, the likelihood of large private capital inflows is low, as potential investors wait to see how the policy and economic environment develops. Any inflows are most likely speculative money that might boost the exchange rate but create little productive capacity. Longer-term investment prospects are influenced by making profitable investments. This, in turn, is influenced by the probabilities of social and political peace. An overly harsh bargain to compel macroeconomic stability does not attract investors. The IMF recognized this by the late 1990s and now is more discriminating in its policy recommendations and the design of its aid packages.

Currency defense: the attempt by monetary authorities to maintain the foreign exchange value of the home currency.

Choosing a Regime

No one exchange rate regime is always appropriate, and the choice of regime must be based on observant pragmatism, not on dogmatic adherence to a rule. Different violence-afflicted states have chosen different avenues, from dollarization (the adoption of another state's currency) to dual-currency systems to flexible rates to interventionist managed floats. The presence of currency black markets usually is a good indicator that an undue policy is being followed. Likewise, large speculative currency flows—betting for or against a particular currency—can indicate that policy adjustments may be needed.

Violence and Global Financial Markets

Beyond general mechanics and considerations, there are two specific causal connections between violence and exchange rate movements, running in both directions. Perhaps the best-known case is that of the 1997 East Asian financial crisis, during which vast speculative currency movements destabilized entire economies, especially in Indonesia, Malaysia, the Philippines, Thailand, and South Korea. Currency speculation, like many other forms of speculation, works essentially on expectations. Suppose that the exchange rate of the Thai baht (THB) to the U.S. dollar is THB10/USD1 and also that speculators expect the rate to change to THB20/USD1. A dollar bought by selling ten baht now can be sold again for twenty baht if the expectation comes true. If the expectations turn out to be wrong, the speculators lose money; the business risk is quite real. But if many speculators, sharing the same expectation, start selling baht to snap up dollars cheaply, they drive down the value of the baht. The expectation becomes a self-fulfilling prophecy, and the baht collapses.

The problem lies not so much in currency depreciation or appreciation as in the rapidity of the changes. A speculative attack that drives the baht down in value increases, for example, the cost of needed imports. While the depreciation should also make tourist visits and exports cheaper, economies cannot adjust quickly enough to take advantage of this; they cannot reallocate labor and production resources the very instant the currency markets heave. To deal with the extraordinary harm that can be done by the divergence between the physical economy and the financial economy, governments sometimes try to countermand currency movements. In the case of the Thai baht during the financial crisis, this meant meeting the speculative selling of baht by buying them, with dollars from the central bank's foreign currency holdings. When these holdings—needed to pay for imports—are depleted, the currency defense has to be abandoned, and the currency collapses, taking the domestic economy with it.

Why would speculators attack a currency in the first place? Why do they form expectations about a currency one way or another? Regarding Thailand, the view developed that the country had taken on too much real estate–related, U.S. dollar–denominated debt. At the time, the actual exchange was a fixed rate of THB25/USD1. In the belief that this fixed rate could not be maintained, speculators sold baht and bought dollars. The speculators were correct: The Thai government did not and could not defend its currency indefinitely as it ran down its reserves of nearly USD50 billion. The currency was floated and eventually dropped to THB56/USD1, less than half its precrisis value. (It has recovered since.) The IMF poured in billions of dollars in loans to the Thai government to play against the speculators, who then left the currency alone because, in principle, the IMF pockets are very deep and the stakes can be raised. Speculators are not in business to lose money. But the damage was done. With the collapse of its dollar-pegged currency in July 1997, a vast financial and economic collapse ensued, unleashing political tensions and the potential for violence that have not subsided to this day. The Thai government faltered; a new constitution, long in preparation, was introduced in October 1997, but then abrogated during a military coup in 2006.

In Malaysia, a vast economic crisis took hold within days of the Thai currency crisis. This resulted in a nasty political struggle over economic policy differences between Malaysia's ruler and its finance minister, a struggle also not settled to this day. While mass violence did not occur in Thailand or Malaysia, the related currency collapse in Indonesia was directly associated with the end of the Suharto regime in 1998, the beginning of the violent secession of Timor-Leste in 1999, and the atrocious civil war that followed there and in the northwestern province of Aceh as well.

The opposite direction of causation, from violence and war to currency collapse, has already been noted—for example, in Zimbabwe, but also in Germany following the failure to reconstitute its economy after World War I. Even for the less spectacularly catastrophic cases of the United States' post–World War II conflicts, from Korea to Afghanistan, the value of the U.S. currency—and with it, the economic effects through foreign trade on the domestic economy—appears to suffer regularly with the onset and conduct of war.[16] Financial historians point to the development of the domestic and global bond market as intricately linked to the need to finance war.[17] To finance war-related spending, governments can cut nonwar spending or print money, which is inflationary. Neither option is attractive and, in quick-thinking democracies at least, voters will not like either of them. Alternatively, governments can sell war bonds, borrowing money domestically. Voters gamble on them, in essence betting their savings that their government will win the war and eventually repay the borrowed funds with interest. But governments can also raise bond money from abroad. The financing for the U.S. wars in Afghanistan and Iraq in the 2000s largely came from China. As the United States runs a very large trade deficit with China, the dollars that China earns are plowed back into the U.S. financial markets, from which the U.S. government borrows to plug its gaping federal government budget deficit. Much of China's dollar reserves are held in sovereign wealth funds (SWFs). If China were to decide to sell off its massive dollar holdings, the U.S. currency would be massively devalued. This danger is countered only by China's self-interest not to undermine the value of these holdings. As with private business speculators, there is no reason why China would want to lose money. But even an orderly unloading of dollars, or a shift by China into currency holdings other than U.S. dollars, would put downward pressure on the dollar—and upward pressure on the currencies China moved into.

Institutions and Policies

In addition to the IMF and World Bank, a number of global trade and finance institutions, both public and private (formal and informal), have roles to play in creating and resolving conflict. Formed in 1995 and headquartered in Geneva, the WTO is an international organization composed of member states that have signed and ratified various legally binding agreements regarding their conduct in the international trade of goods and services and the protection of intellectual property rights. The WTO secretariat administers trade agreements, serves as a forum for trade negotiations, operates a well-used dispute settlement mechanism (over three hundred cases in its first ten years of existence), reviews members' trade policies, and provides technical assistance and support to emerging and developing economies. By mid-July 2008, 153 states were members and about thirty more were negotiating accession. On its website, the WTO makes explicit reference to negotiation and peaceful dispute resolution to reduce the risk of "military conflict."[18]

To promote trade while extricating themselves from their own overly complex regulations, many states have set up special economic zones (SEZs), or export processing (EPZs) or free trade zones (FTZs). These economic experiments are specific to location, product, or industry. Forms of governance range from fully public to fully private and any mix in between. Shenzhen in China and Subic Bay in the Philippines are prominent examples. Many countries have multiple such zones, India in particular. As establishing an SEZ means acquiring special physical sites and constructing appropriate transportation and other infrastructure, conflict with local communities, including violent conflict, can emerge. A prominent case involved Tata Motors of India, which had planned to locate a production facility for its Nano automobile in the Singur SEZ. Disputes over land acquisition, population displacement, fair land compensation, and other issues led Tata to abandon the project in late 2008 and to locate elsewhere in India.

The Extractive Industries Transparency Initiative (EITI) is a very different type of institution, an attempt to bring transparency and accountability to the billions of dollars generated in the global trade of raw materials extracted from Earth. This stemmed, in part, from a publish-what-you-pay campaign that sought to compel companies to publish the sums paid to states for natural resource extraction (natural resource rents) so that government use of these funds could be tracked and corruption and fund mismanagement reduced. The development of a Natural Resource Charter has followed—"a set of economic principles for governments and societies on how to best manage the opportunities created by natural resources for development"[19]—that involves Ernesto Zedillo, former president of Mexico and now an economics professor at Yale University; Michael Spence, an economics Nobel laureate and professor at Stanford University; and Paul Collier, an economist at Oxford University and former director of development research at the World Bank.

On the financial side, the Bank for International Settlement (BIS), headquartered in Basel, serves as a bank for central banks. Formed in 1930, it describes itself as "the world's oldest international financial organization." Its original function was to collect, administer, and distribute reparation payments imposed on Germany with the Treaty of Versailles following

World War I. Since then, it has moved into statistics gathering, research, and policy deliberation, advice, and coordination for central bankers. The bank's work is never far removed from considerations of the links between violence and the economy. A 2007 BIS working paper shows the drastic, permanent economic dislocation caused by financial crises, wars, and civil wars.[20] Its authors find that the failure of emerging and developing economies to converge to the level of advanced economies can be wholly explained by the frequency and severity of such crises. The policy implication clearly relates to crisis prevention or, at least, avoidance.

In the wake of the finance-induced global economic crisis of 2009, researchers and policymakers have sought to reform the global financial architecture—in part in conjunction with the BIS—and, with it, to broaden global macroeconomic and financial policy coordination. This harks back to the mid-1970s, when, at the invitation of the then president of France, Valéry Giscard d'Estaing, an informal gathering of the leaders of France, Germany, Italy, Japan, the United Kingdom, and the United States, soon joined by Canada, evolved into an annual Group of Seven (G7) economic policy coordination meeting. Later, Russia, the European Union, and representatives of international financial institutions joined the meeting. In September 2009, at the Pittsburgh meeting of the G7, the gathering was opened up to the Group of 20 (G20), a group that includes Brazil, China, India, Indonesia, Mexico, South Africa, and others. It had become clear enough that the relative economic heft of the G7 had lessened and that policy coordination required talks among an expanded set of participants.

As billions of people still have no access to banking services, informal financial networks are extensive. Because they are informal, they can and have been abused to move illicitly gained funds or funds intended for illicit purposes. The Financial Action Task Force (FATF), established as one outcome of the 1989 G7 meeting, is an intergovernmental body, headquartered in Paris, "whose purpose is the development and promotion of national and international policies to combat money laundering and terrorist financing." It has produced nearly fifty recommendations that effectively serve as performance standards for its over thirty state members. In April 2009, FATF published an anti–money laundering (AML) and counterterrorist financing (CTF) evaluation and assessment handbook for countries and assessors. Assessment teams have visited members to evaluate and assess compliance with the FATF standards. The resulting reports are publicly available on the FATF website.

Although FATF deals in part with informal and illegal money flows, many of its recommendations pertain to local, national, and supranational laws, rules, and effective enforcement regarding commercial banking; certainly the very large global financial firms have participated and cooperated in FATF's work. One of the challenges concerns how to deal with truly globe-spanning giant corporations, as the sum of their intrafirm activity accounts for a large fraction of global trade and financial flows. Complicity in, or at least insensitivity to, human rights abuses is alleged, and sometimes documented, both for wholly private corporations as well as for state-run companies (e.g., Chinese companies in Africa). But on the whole, companies and their suppliers, employees, and customers are victims of violence much more often than they are perpetrators. They much prefer to deal with single, universal standards rather than with a multiplicity of standard setters, standards, and costly audits. Businesses speak of audit fatigue as they try to comply with numerous mandatory and voluntary local, national, and global standards issued by different agencies and authorities. Yet much of the business world still approaches peace and security solely from a risk and liability management perspective rather than from a more engaged and forward-looking violence prevention and avoidance perspective. The documented risk of civil war relapse should encourage both peace negotiators and major corporations, or councils of corporations, to talk to each other before a peace deal is signed.

FAILURE AND SUCCESS: Two Case Studies

FAILURE: FIJI

For nearly one hundred years, from 1874 to 1970, the United Kingdom was Fiji's colonial overlord. To work Fijian sugar fields, Britain moved contract labor to the islands from India; by the early 2000s, over 40 percent of the population was of Indian descent. This planted the seeds of post-independence ethnic-based strife on the islands. Two coups in 1987 unseated then recently elected ethnic Indian–dominated governments. Subsequently, tens of thousands of Fijians of Indian heritage emigrated, leaving the economy short of skilled labor, adversely affecting labor productivity. The political uncertainties resulting from the 1987 coups were not settled until 1997. During this time military expenditure absorbed at times well over 10 percent of the annual government budget, artificially boosting GDP. In

FIGURE 4.1. Fiji, 1960–2009

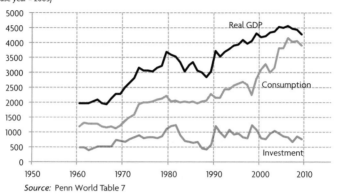

Inflation, population, and purchasing
power parity–adjusted per capita
GDP, consumption, and investment
(I$, base year = 2005)

Source: Penn World Table 7

2000 another coup occurred, resulting in international economic and political penalties, including trade barriers for this trade-dependent state. Exchange rate and price controls further discouraged trade and FDI. In 2005
unrest arose again, resulting in yet another coup in 2006. Today, uncertainties remain with regard to land tenure and other issues, and the political
situation is ultimately unresolved.

The islands of Fiji are small and distant, implying insufficient economies
of scale for domestic manufacturing. Its near neighbors also are distant and
small islands, with the same economies of scale problems. Thus, both local
and neighborhood trade effects are small. Distances to the continents are
large and imply high transportation costs for exports and imports and impede industrial diversification. Consequently, Fiji's economy is natural resource–based, mostly in tourism, fisheries, forest products, and commercial
agriculture—especially the export-dependent sugarcane sector—and some
mining, notably of gold deposits. Civil strife, violence, and war accentuate
these natural difficulties.

With collapsing investment, Fiji's economy declined for about seven
years before the 1987 coups. The economy is generally subject to sharp
swings in performance (see figure 4.1). Declining sugar prices despite
subsidies offered by the European Union, drastic fluctuations in tourist revenues even when that sector was shored up with periodic currency devalu-
ations aimed at the Australian and New Zealand tourist markets, low
and declining FDI, and continuous skilled labor emigration explain Fiji's

uninspiring economic performance in the 2000s. Figure 4.1 shows clearly that while the level of investment increased during the 1960s and 1970s and into the early 1980s, it has not recovered. The share of investment in GDP is declining, slowly eroding the country's physical asset base. That GDP and consumption appear to have risen since 1990 is due to military expenditure, the taking on of unsustainable debt, and the periodic bolstering of the fickle tourism trade. Neither the fiscal nor the monetary policy stance of the current government is sustainable. Annual budget deficits and cumulative debt are very high, and a much-needed structural reform and diversification of the economy has not happened. Debasing the currency to attract tourists and foster relatively low-value-added exports instead of seeking currency stability and investment in human and public and private physical capital to increase productivity has proved to be an inappropriate and inadequate economic strategy.

SUCCESS: VIETNAM

In contrast to Fiji, Vietnam has been much more economically stable and successful in recent years. War in Vietnam had lasted for over a century, going back to the 1860s, when the country became a French plantation colony. Independence struggles, the two world wars, and two follow-on wars lasted until 1976 with the conclusion of the second Indochina war. By then, millions of people were injured or dead or, as in Fiji, had left the country, leading to a depletion of labor resources. Vietnam invaded Cambodia in 1978 and was itself briefly invaded by China in 1979, so that the war period did not end until that year.

By 1980, when Vietnam's wars had ended, political, economic, and cultural reunification proved difficult and led to few economic advances. Fiji's per capita GDP (I$3,593) was nearly six times as large as Vietnam's (I$657). But by 2009, the roughly I$3,000 gap had been cut in half to about I$1,500. Moreover, whereas in 1980, Fiji's GDP composition showed some balance between investment and consumption while Vietnam's was all consumption (that is, asset depletion or debt accumulation via borrowing), by 2009 the situation had reversed: Vietnam is balanced and Fijians live on borrowed money.

Vietnam's transition from war-induced devastation to relative success was not automatic. As figure 4.2 shows, the improvement in the country's economic fortunes began not in 1976 but 1990. In 1986 Vietnam's leadership—as in China beforehand—approved the introduction of a socialist-

FIGURE 4.2. Vietnam, 1970–2009

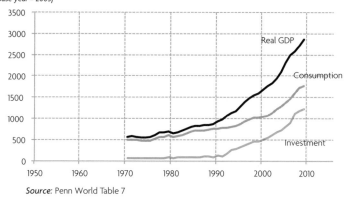

Inflation, population, and purchasing
power parity–adjusted per capita
GDP, consumption, and investment
(I$, base year = 2005)

Source: Penn World Table 7

oriented version of free market economics. Structural reform took place amid economic diversification across agriculture, industry, and services, making the country less vulnerable to shocks in any one sector. The end of the Cold War and the subsequent boom in globalization added their own fortunate impetus. Coffee cultivation and exports grew, as did the production and export of cashews, rice, black pepper, and other agricultural products. Even so, FDI in low-skill manufacturing as well as in high-skill, high-technology fields has proved very attractive, sustained, and successful, so that the share of agriculture in GDP has declined and that of industry has increased. Rural labor resources migrate to urban centers, where industrial development has been able to absorb them, at least in economic terms. More recently, offshore oil exploration has commenced. Thus, even though it depends heavily on international trade and finance, Vietnam has done much better in this regard than has Fiji.

Vietnam's recent success is driven by its domestic, neighborhood, and global trade opportunities. This is likely to continue as Chinese wages and manufacturing costs rise and contract manufacturing shifts south to Vietnam. But it took a long-delayed political decision to enable these opportunities to come to the fore. The 1997 East Asian financial crisis that devastated Indonesia, Thailand, and other states in the region had little effect on Vietnam's economy. Undoubtedly, as with the predemocratic regimes in Hong Kong, Singapore, South Korea, and Taiwan in the 1970s, political stability, combined with an economic opening, is a key factor explaining the attraction of private business interests to Vietnam. That said, across a range of global rankings, such as competitiveness, human development, ease of doing business, economic freedom, perception of corruption, and other indices, Vietnam does not rank high. This suggests that its economy is riding along a narrow channel of politically facilitated trade opportunities that may not take an independent and sustainable hold. By late 2007 about 40 percent of GDP was still generated through state-owned enterprises (SOEs). Vietnam's leaders have done an admirable job of controlled economic growth aimed at securing economic and social stability, but a potential downside is that of inadvertently maneuvering into an economic corner where policy flexibility is restricted to a set of unpalatable options.

Policy Lessons and Tips

LESSON 4.1: The effects of war, civil war, and crime affect a country's balance of payments, the value of its currency, and its trade position, and therefore inflation, employment, and economic growth.

LESSON 4.2: Voluntary trade is mutually beneficial, both within and across borders.

LESSON 4.3: Statistics from the WTO reveal two important facts. First, international merchandise trade is dominated by neighborhood effects (intraregional trade) and this, in turn, is highly correlated to transport infrastructure. Second, world trade in manufactured items has grown much faster than trade in fuels and mining products, which, in turn, have grown slightly faster than trade in agricultural products. Both facts bode ill for landlocked, violence-affected states with poor infrastructure and relatively unskilled populations. Shortcomings in these areas need to be rectified quickly.

LESSON 4.4: There is no inevitable natural resource curse, but failure to diversify can create undue and fragile natural resource dependency that can be a focal point of violent conflict.

LESSON 4.5: Foreign aid is small relative to workers' remittances and FDI. Freeing global trade from protectionism would release far more aid to violence-afflicted states than does ODA.

LESSON 4.6: There is no one right foreign exchange regime for all situations. Proper currency management is important to guard against black currency markets or speculative currency attacks, which can plunge states into episodes of severe violence.

LESSON 4.7: The connections between violence and currencies are surprisingly deep. They can foment decades-long economic decline and cause conflict to explode with a suddenness and rapidity against which there is virtually no defense other than foresight and preventive anticipation.

LESSON 4.8: Very many public, private, and public-private global organizations exist in the field of international trade and finance. With the exception of the IMF and the World Bank, they have not, on the whole, directly engaged with the topic of interpersonal and collective violence. They should.

Notes

1. To use another example, German machine tools exported to Mexico would earn the German exporter Mexican pesos. But the exporter needs euros to pay its employees and local suppliers. Thus, the pesos will be sold for euros. The buyer, say the European Central Bank, now holds the pesos, but they are best invested back in Mexican government bonds, for instance, so as to earn some interest. Alternatively, another company can buy the pesos, maybe a company that purchases Mexican products and needs to pay the Mexican producer in pesos. Even if the pesos are handed off several times, ultimately they will end up back in Mexico.

2. World Trade Organization (WTO), *International Trade Statistics 2007* (Geneva: WTO, 2007), 2–3.

3. The UNDP's list is somewhat shorter: "Risk factors include low per capita income, weak economic growth, the presence of socioeconomic horizontal inequalities, and abundant high-value natural resources. These risk factors are even more acute in the presence of high unemployment, especially among youth." See UNDP, *Post-Conflict Economic Recovery,* 17.

4. For a recent substantial review on the economics of natural resources, see F. van der Ploeg, "Natural Resources: Curse or Blessing?" *Journal of Economic Literature,* vol. 49, no. 2 (2011), 366–420.

5. See Anderton and Carter, *Principles of Conflict Economics,* on the cost of trade interruption in war; see Polachek, "How Trade Affects International Transactions," on the peace-and-trade hypothesis and evidence.

6. N. Cooper, "Peaceful Warriors and Warring Peacemakers," *The Economics of Peace and Security Journal,* vol. 1, no. 1 (2006), 20–24.

7. N. Cooper, "On Forgetful Goldfish and Failed Mnemonics: Transforming Political Economies of Conflict Using Voluntarism, Regulation, and Supervision," *The Economics of Peace and Security Journal,* vol. 5, no. 1 (2010), 43–51. On nondiamond jewelry, especially gold, see J. Tepper-Marlin, "The 'No Dirty-Gold' Campaign: What Economists Can Learn from and Contribute to Corporate Campaigns," *The Economics of Peace and Security Journal,* vol. 1, no. 2 (2006), 58–64. See also Global Witness, "Global Witness Leaves Kimberley Process, Calls for Diamond Trade to Be Held Accountable," December 5, 2011, available at http://www.globalwitness.org/library/global-witness-leaves-kimberley-process-calls-diamond-trade-be-held-accountable (accessed January 29, 2012).

8. See OECD, "Development Co-operation Report."

9. UNDP, *Post-Conflict Economic Recovery,* 86.

10. See UNCTAD, *World Investment Report 2009.*

11. See WTO, *World Trade Report* (Geneva: WTO, 2006); for PSE figures, 123; for U.S. figures, 128, Table 11; for EU-15 figures, 131, Table 12.

12. The probability of war renewal is between 25 and 50 percent; UNDP, *Post-Conflict Economic Recovery,* 16.

13. Alternatively, the exchange rate can be set by law. This amounts to an explicit price control and encourages the development of a black market in which currency is privately traded, albeit illegally.

14. Over the years, a number of other states have joined, left, and rejoined the CFA currency areas. In 2009, in addition to the former French colonies—Cameroon, the Central African Republic, Chad, the Republic of the Congo, and Gabon in Central Africa and Benin, Burkina Faso, Côte d'Ivoire, Mali, Niger, Senegal, and Togo in West Africa—the CFA was also used by the former Portuguese colony of Guinea-Bissau (Central CFA) and the former Spanish colony of Equatorial Guinea (West CFA). Although the exchange value is fixed, the Central and West African CFAs are not mutually recognized.

15. Despite the availability of ample case material, the relation among currency, explicit or implicit (through fixed exchange rates) currency unions, and violence is not well investigated in the economics literature. The post–World War II Bretton Woods system created a system of fixed exchange rates. The political, cultural, and economic development of today's European Union is strongly tied to currency regimes, including the creation of the euro. Under apartheid, the southern African customs union also included a currency union in which states such as Lesotho and Swaziland handed control over monetary policy and over export and import regimes to South Africa.

16. On the value of the U.S. dollar and U.S. wars through history, see C.E.S. Warburton, "War and Exchange Rate Valuation," *The Economics of Peace and Security Journal,* vol. 4, no. 1 (2009), 62–69.

17. See N. Ferguson, *The Ascent of Money: A Financial History of the World* (New York: Penguin Books, 2008).

18. "The result [of the WTO's existence] is . . . a more prosperous, peaceful and accountable economic world. Virtually all decisions in the WTO are taken by consensus among all member countries and they are ratified by members' parliaments. Trade friction is channelled into the WTO's dispute settlement process where the focus is on interpreting agreements and commitments, and how to ensure that countries' trade policies conform with them. That way, the risk of disputes spilling over into political or military conflict is reduced. By lowering trade barriers, the WTO's system also breaks down other barriers between peoples and nations." See WTO, "The WTO in Brief," available at http://www.wto.org/english/thewto_e/whatis_e/inbrief_e/inbr00_e.htm (accessed December 6, 2011).

19. Bank for International Settlements, "BIS History—Overview," available at http://www.bis.org/about/history.htm (accessed January 29, 2012).

20. Cerra and Saxena, "Growth Dynamics."

5

DESIGNING AND PROMOTING PEACE

Of conflicts that have ended since 1989, those that ended in peace agreements have a considerably lower rate of [war] recurrence (14 percent) than the overall rate of 47 percent. Conflicts that ended in outright victory for one side had a recurrence rate of 45 percent, and all of those with an ambiguous ending recurred. This is consistent with other findings which show that peace accords supported by the United Nations and generous development assistance produce better outcomes than military victories alone.
—UNDP[1]

War recurrence—or war after war—is common. Estimates suggest that one-fifth to one-half of all concluded recent civil wars restart within a few years' time. Recidivism is high.[2] Risk factors for war recurrence that need to be addressed in the design of peace include "low per capita income, weak economic growth, the presence of socioeconomic horizontal inequalities and abundant high-value natural resources . . . [even more so] in the presence of high unemployment, especially among youth."[3] Horizontal inequality—inequality among culturally distinct groups rather than within them—depends on

how inclusive the post-conflict political system is; whether or not conflict itself has remedied such inequalities, as in the case of successful ethnoregional secession; whether or not previously excluded or marginalized groups or regions have gained more equitable economic and political standing from peace agreements and their implementation; whether prior injustices associated with real and perceived discrimination against an aggrieved group are satisfactorily addressed; [and] how the dynamics of inter-group relations are affected by the conditions of post-conflict peacebuilding and development.[4]

Peace treaties should do more than pay homage to the free market and refer to a sound, stable, public sector–enabled macroeconomic framework. These things themselves need to be placed within a higher-order level of economic principles of institutional or treaty design. Third-party intervention through diplomatic, military, or foreign aid channels is not always for the better. Third parties have vested interests that can affect these designs, possibly to the detriment of peace.

The Economics of Design

Some fields of economics deal with societal institutions, their design, and their mechanics.[5] These have been employed to create revenue-maximizing auctions, by which a government allocates, say, portions of the electromagnetic spectrum for use to competing cell phone, radio, and television companies. The design of default options is another example. In the U.S. retirement system, most employees whose companies offer retirement contribution benefits have to opt into the benefit plan. If they do, a portion of their income is placed into tax-advantaged stock, bond, real estate, or other funds of their choosing, as is an additional amount from the employer. If a specific employee does not opt in, the paycheck is not reduced, but the employer also does not contribute. As it turns out, under an opt-in requirement, a surprisingly large percentage of employees fail to do so: They forgo the steady accumulation of retirement savings, tax advantages, and contributions from their employers. If, however, the design is changed so that employees must opt out, most employees again fail to do so. Simple inertia or default options appear to explain people's choice behavior.[6]

Choice architecture: the self-conscious and deliberate design of incentives that inhibit undesired and promote desired individual behavior, such that a social system as a whole moves toward a desired outcome.

Rent seeking: generating unearned income by seeking to rewrite political, economic, and cultural rules in one's favor rather than earning income through fair competitive and productive effort.

Similarly, one challenge of peace economics is to understand both peace failures and successes from a design perspective—what in the field of industrial organization is referred to as the structure, conduct, and performance triplet, or rules, strategies, and outcomes—and to invent new mechanisms to arrive at stable peace within and between societies. Structure, or choice architecture, as Thaler and Sunstein call it,[7] refers to the deliberate design of incentives that inhibit undesired and promote desired individual behavior, guiding the choices people make so that a social system as a whole moves toward a desired outcome. For the retirement example, a simple switch from opt-in to opt-out contract provisions changes choices, getting the desired outcome of more people saving for their retirement years.

From a design perspective, it becomes clear why people, firms, parties, or vested interests jostle to massage the rules and why influence seeking, lobbying, rent seeking, bribery, and corruption are so widespread. There is a powerfully compelling logic in the chain that, read backward, says that social outcomes are generated by aggregations of individual behaviors, and that these, in turn, stem from the ground rules. The difficulty lies not in understanding people's behavior—there is no question that people respond to incentives—but in understanding which rules and combinations of rules lead to which behavioral responses by large numbers of interacting, self-interested parties, and with which ultimate outcomes. The problem is complex, especially in social systems, where deliberate experimentation is difficult or impossible to carry out.

It can be and has been argued that human history contains a set of giant natural experiments regarding the design of peace, that certain lessons have been learned from the politically, culturally, and economically successful societies that have emerged from these natural experiments, and that these lessons amalgamate today into cries for democracy, the rule of law, and free market economics.[8] Even so, the quality of these outcomes varies across societies, leading to the question of what the structural differences are that produce durable and stable peace in one place and not in another.[9] We are searching for a kind of market regulation, a setting down of mutually agreed-upon, enforceable rules by which society lives, a reconstruction of a social contract. What are the key elements in the design of a stable peace?

The Social Contract and the Economics of Designing Peace

As discussed in chapter 1, although there is neither an agreed-upon definition nor a measurement of social capital, it can be viewed as an asset that consists of the social and communal networks humans build. Social capital may find expression in formal and informal institutions and their products (e.g., bank notes), but it is more akin to intangibles such as trust between and among members of a community and toward strangers.[10] Together, these networks represent a stock of achievements that, once destroyed, can be extremely difficult to rebuild. In their absence, production, markets, and income-earning opportunities diminish.

Today, virtually all societies use fiat money, inherently worthless pieces of paper that become valuable not on the say-so of a governing authority but on the large-scale acceptance of those who use it. The community endows money with value. This makes money a social fiction, a communal faith, or a "collective thought," as contemporary Buddhist philosopher Ken McLeod calls it.[11] If the faith in money wavers, people flee into other assets, such as precious metals—gold in particular. Hence the fearful specter of hyperinflation: Once faith in the value of money is lost, no seller wants to receive it, even as buyers inundate them with it. The economy simultaneously overflows with and runs out of its most important lubricant. And war economies tend to suffer from inflation and the loss of collective faith in the affected currency more than do peaceful economies.

Social contract: a framework of widely agreed-upon rules of social cohesion and trust, along with external or self-policing enforcing institutions.

The social contract lies at the base of collective thought and social capital. Mansoob Murshed observes that "some societies despite having conditions predisposing them to civil war, such as horizontal inequality, polarization, and natural resource rents, do not descend into conflict," and that behind a veil of surface factors "other factors [are] at work, specifically a weakening of what may be described as the social contract following classical thinkers such as Hobbes, Locke, and Rousseau among others." He continues:

Even if rents from capturable resources do constitute a sizeable prize, violent conflict is unlikely to take hold if a country has a framework of widely agreed rules, both formal and informal, that govern the allocation of resources, including resource rents, and the peaceful settlement of grievances. A viable social contract can be sufficient to restrain, if not eliminate, opportunistic behavior such as large-scale theft of resource rents, and the violent expression of grievance.[12]

What is required, then, is the reconstitution of "a framework of widely agreed rules," of social cohesion, of an economy of trust, and of trust in trust-enforcing institutions. Murshed connects the quality of social contract to economic achievement:

> Higher per capita income implies a better functioning social contract, institutions, and state capacity. Yet economic development, even if it eventually diminishes motives for conflict, may at first increase violence in poor institutional settings, if growth is not pro-poor and disadvantages some groups.[13]

The World Bank's *World Development Report 2011* has endorsed these views in its call for peace, justice, and jobs, noting that such work requires the reconstitution of people's confidence and trust in social institutions. But neither Murshed's article nor the Bank's *Report* are particularly specific on the enabling policy conditions for a social contract. In the pages that follow, we lay out some relevant principles that designers of peace agreements should not fail to meet. They cannot guarantee peace, but they can make failure less likely.

Systems control theory suggests three requirements for economic design:[14] There must be agreement on goals, there must be ways to measure goal compliance or deviation, and there must exist a correction mechanism. This is the triplet of goals, feedback, and enforcement. The types of institutions needed to prevent system failure are also known. The crucial question is how to construct these institutions so that they fulfill their intended function. In principle, private markets provide these institutions, but it turns out that peacemaking and peacekeeping are subject to severe market failure; hence the need to think about the construction of collective institutions to deliver peace services—which, evidently, also can fail.

The twelve design principles in building peace institutions described below, if followed, should explain the successful making and the resilient keeping of peace.[15] Conversely, their absence or violation should explain the continuance or recurrence of war. Applying selected principles will diminish prospects for peace: The principles—steps toward a choice architecture of peace—should be viewed as a complete and mutually reinforcing package. Indeed, they serve as the basis for defining peace economics as "the economic study and design of political, economic, and cultural

> *Peace economics:* the economic study and design of political, economic, and cultural institutions, their interrelations, and their policies to prevent, mitigate, or resolve any type of latent or actual violence or other destructive conflict within and between societies.

institutions, their interrelations, and their policies to prevent, mitigate, or resolve any type of latent or actual violence or other destructive conflict within and between societies."[16]

The Principle of Changing Payoffs

To induce people toward cooperative action, one must minimize incentives to defect and maximize incentives to cooperate. A number of wars have been prolonged because of strong incentives to defect from peace negotiations. In Angola in the 1990s, the ability of the National Union for the Total Independence of Angola (UNITA) to mine and sell raw diamonds created cash flow. Similarly, the Angolan government's ability to extract and sell crude oil kept it well financed. Both sides were flush with money and had no financial reason to settle. By contrast, in Mozambique, both sides settled when they did run out of money.[17] The ability to change payoffs can change conflicting parties' behavior. The design of peace agreement must therefore be calibrated to align incentives and payoffs toward cooperation.

The Principle of Creating Vested Interests and Leadership

If two players cannot change the relevant payoffs themselves, an external force—a leader—may need to intervene. A leader is an actor able to organize changes in the payoff structure or the rules of the game. This can be done by, say, contributing or denying superior military intelligence and arms to one side to force another side to offer negotiation. It can also be done by withholding existing support to impose the cost of fighting on both parties.[18] But leaders often are not neutral (see below) and need to be rewarded with their own positive payoffs; why else would a leader intervene?[19] In Rwanda, little was done in 1994 until after several hundred thousand people had been killed. There was no sufficient vested interest to prevent the budding crisis: The war had been going on since 1990. By contrast, in the early 1990s, when large numbers of Haitian refugees arrived on Florida's shores, the U.S. government intervened because it had a vested interest in keeping people out of the United States. Similarly, in the Balkan wars of the 1990s, the initial vested interest was to contain the slaughter to the Balkans: When large numbers of refugees spilled into the richer, West European nations, and when there was a danger of the violence spreading throughout the neighborhood, the European Union—and ultimately the North Atlantic Treaty Organization (NATO)—intervened. Thus, one way to foster peace is to deliberately engineer and trigger preventive rather than curative vested interests.[20]

The Principle of Graduated Reciprocity and Clarity

Research has shown that a tit-for-tat strategy can be highly successful and stable. Suppose there are two players, A and B. In the first interaction A cooperates with B. Thereafter, A always copies what B does in the prior round of play. If B cooperates, so will A in the next round. If B defects from cooperation, so will A in the next round. If B makes a concession, so will A; if B fails to make a follow-on concession, so will A. This strategy's unmistakable clarity and automaticity build reputation effects and credible commitments to cooperate. Either way, for B there is no second-guessing about what A will do. Moreover, the tit-for-tat strategy holds no grudge and forgives a past defection: Party A readily resumes cooperation once party B cooperates again. However, if B misunderstands or mistrusts A, it can set in motion a series of mutual defections. Thus, scholars recommend that A assume a graduated response strategy and show limited capacity to be provoked if it is interested in peace. This means that if B defects, so will A, but by something less than full defection. If B fails to make a follow-on concession, A offers only a minor follow-on concession in turn. If B then continues to defect, A gradually moves toward full defection also. Thus all the benefits to be had from cooperation are party B's to lose.

A nongraduated response appeared in the Libyan uprising in spring and summer of 2011, with the refusal of Libya's leader, Muammar Gadhafi, to resign from power. Given the design of the options, Gadhafi could either fight to the death or face capture and trial before the International Criminal Court (ICC) in The Hague. No doubt anticipating the adverse outcome of a trial, Gadhafi continued to fight, with horrible consequences for the peace and welfare of the Libyan people. A graduated response might have offered an exit option of exile in another country. If Gadhafi had not accepted, then the stronger response could have been played. But the design of the ICC statues no longer permits the exile option, as the court's member states are obligated to capture and turn over indicted persons.

The Principle of Repeated, Small Steps

Instead of a single, comprehensive peace negotiation, it may be more effective to have many smaller negotiations. This increases the frequency of meetings and the duration of the overall interaction, which poses risks to success. But if a small round can be brought to a cooperative outcome, both sides then risk losing gains already obtained and forfeiting future gains if they fail to continue to cooperate. Contrast the lack of progress in the all-or-nothing approach to the Israeli-Arab conflict with the formation and gradual expansion of what eventually became the European Union. The former approach sometimes can be a ploy to prevent negotiations from succeeding.

The Principle of Common Value Formation

In a 1978 book of essays, Thomas Schelling reports on a game he played with his children.[21] He took a checkerboard, populated it with a random but thorough mix of black-colored and white-colored pieces, and left a few squares empty so that pieces could be moved about. He then stipulated a rule that pieces preferred to be surrounded by some minimum number of same-colored pieces; that is, each piece tended toward some neighborhood mixing, but not to the extent that the neighborhood could become dominated by opposite-colored pieces. The rule determined the maximum degree of acceptable homogeneity: For instance, for a center piece, no more than five out of eight neighbors could be of the opposite color, and for an edge piece, no more than three out of five. If a space exceeded this limit, then the piece in question was moved to an empty space where the rule could be met. For each of a number of varying degrees of homogeneity, Schelling found that after a series of moves to meet the rule, distinctly black and white neighborhoods developed. What appears to be forced segregation may be the outcome of voluntary aggregation: Like and like attract each other, and when they do, they appear to form opposing groups.

If one can change the pieces' preferences, however—say, so that each piece thinks of itself as gray—then any degree of mixing is acceptable and moves happen for reasons other than color (or identity). In short, one needs to find and foster that which binds conflicting parties rather than that which divides them.[22] Forming common preferences that transcend other types of differences produces voluntary aggregations of like-minded actors who are likely to cooperate for mutual benefit. This applies to individuals,

groups, and states, and can account for the proclamations of former ene-
mies who, during negotiations, learn that they share values such as leadership, political savvy, and care for their respective citizens, and end up with
personal respect for each other.[23] This principle also explains why culturally similar nations tend to cooperate well, disagreements notwithstanding.
Similarities in political and economic systems, religious beliefs, language,
and cultural heritage do not guarantee but tend to forge reliable bonds
across states to form clusters of cooperative behavior. Large group size by
itself does not necessarily make collective action on common value formation impossible; neither does small group size always promote it.

The Principle of Authentic Authority

Those affected by a collective action—negotiating a peace agreement involves multiple people, and is thus a collective rather than a private action—
must have a voice in shaping the decision. This raises the question of how
peace negotiators derive their authority to speak for others, which leads
into issues of culturally sanctioned forms of representation, the right to organize and assemble, and the ability of people to address their own problems as well as find indigenous solutions to them.[24] Without authentic representation in negotiations, peace may not be stable. Disaffected groups
may continue to fight if they believe that their concerns have not been
heard. To prevent disaffection and violent conflict, majorities may need to
grant minimum rights to others, such as freedom to exercise religious beliefs. Because of the focus on representation, this principle allows for continuous self-transformation of institutions as old problems dissipate and
new problems arise that affected communities need to address. All voices
need to be heard, and satisfactory solutions can be surprisingly varied.[25]

The Principle of Subsidiarity

According to the principle of subsidiarity, problems should be addressed
at the minimum level necessary. Higher-level, external involvement—as
from global institutions—may not be the ideal first response to a problem;[26] many conflicts are best resolved at the local level without involving
an outside intervener at all. The Global Commission on Drug Policy argued in June 2011 that achievement of the 1961 United Nations Single
Convention on Narcotic Drugs, to which member states are legally bound
to adhere, has obstructed experimentation with alternative policies.[27]

Under the convention's current design, a single member can stop progress and prevent changes, even to adapt to changing circumstances. This
violates the principles of subsidiarity: A fifty-year-old superordinate rule
at the UN level restricts what convention members may or may not do to
deal with local realities in limiting the illegal narcotics trade. Changing
the institutional design to accommodate bottom-up experiences through
regular review conferences would be helpful.[28]

The Principle of Conflict Resolution Mechanisms

Peacemaking and peacekeeping rest on agreements, but disagreements
over agreements arise and can lead to resumed conflict. To keep disagreements from escalating, parties must have recourse to conflict resolution
mechanisms such as mediation, arbitration, and a system of courts. The fra-
gility or absence of such mechanisms weakens peacemaking and peacekeeping and increases the likelihood of failure. External interveners can
help provide such mechanisms, as in the legally binding treaty documents
that make up the WTO (see chapter 4), which explicitly mention the organization's dispute-resolution mechanism as a forum to air and settle differences that otherwise might result in recourse to harmful measures. Turkey's continuing exclusion from the European Union and its institutions
serve as a counterexample: Without EU mechanisms to turn to, Greece and
Turkey have one less avenue to address tensions between them—one that
might be handled under the principle of forming common values if Turkey
were to be an EU member. Of course, parties must agree in the first place to
seek external resolution when bilateral talks fail and must be prevented
from reneging. Cambodia and Thailand have fought border skirmishes over
land adjacent to a revered temple site, Preah Vihear, and sought resolution
through presentations at the International Court of Justice in The Hague.
To prevent the parties from reneging, other principles must be in force as
well: Again, the principles do not come singly, but as a package.

The Principle of Information and Monitoring

Information reduces uncertainty, helps create shared values, and leads to
better forecasting of expected benefits and costs as well as behavioral
choices. Misinformation can create uncertainty, false certainty, division of
values, and poorer forecasting. As players may have a vested interest in
creating misinformation, maintaining a diverse, free press is of great im-

portance to assist in peacemaking and peacekeeping. Outside actors can provide additional monitoring; advanced, industrialized countries, for example, have on occasion shared results of their outer space–based satellite monitoring with other states. Such government monitoring, however, is exclusive, as it relies on the self-interest of the government to make the monitoring available. In contrast, commercial satellite networks also can monitor and publicize troop and equipment movements, and their pricing structure is inclusive, in the sense that relevant information can easily be bought and sold. Some may object that involving commercial interests in this way can help entrench repressive governments or help guerrilla movements overthrow legitimate governments. But commercial information is perhaps more likely to encourage negotiation, given that wars are more difficult to win when information about the sides' strengths and movements is readily available.

The Principle of Accountability

Today, it is virtually impossible for leaders to remain anonymous in making war, and with that comes accountability before world opinion. With accurate information, individuals responsible for war actions and war crimes can be identified and named. But mere knowledge of who did what is insufficient. Accountability implies enforcement of the type that is gradually coalescing around the permanent International Criminal Court. Any future warmaker now knows ahead of time that he can be called to account for his actions. Another aspect of accountability links it to the principle of authentic authority: One way to frustrate peace negotiations and prolong violence or war is to send junior officials who are not authorized to make credible, binding commitments, or change negotiators during a negotiation. There must be continuity in representation so that a small set of persons can be held accountable for their actions in negotiations.

The Principle of Self-Policing Enforcement

In the realm of peacemaking and peacekeeping, there are two types of enforcement: external policing and self-policing. External policing suffers from various problems. For example, UN peacekeeping forces are financed on a mission-by-mission basis and are often too late and too weak to intervene effectively in conflicts. Self-policing enforcement is preferable when it can be accomplished, but this requires the right design of incentives so that players prefer to cooperate rather than to defect. One reason why trade is successful is that the prospect of a future trade contract makes parties willing to fulfill the current contract to the satisfaction of the other party. The "shadow of the future" looms large over present behavior.[29] Likewise, self-policing is linked to the monitoring and reciprocity principles. If monitoring shows that player A is cooperating, a self-policing agreement may induce player B to cooperate further, in anticipation of future gains. In this regard, it is generally more efficient and effective to supply parties with the ability to monitor each other than to rely on external monitoring, though there may be exceptions when, for example, economies of scale, or nesting, make it worthwhile to outsource at least part of the monitoring function.

The Principle of Nesting

Economies of scale, scope, and learning may favor nesting institutions that foster coordination and complementarities. The current UN system exemplifies economies of scope, as a large variety of specialized functions are organized under the auspices of an umbrella organization. Peace negotiations are unlikely to show economies of scale—each case is different—but peacekeeping efforts likely do. This suggests the possibility of a standing global peacekeeping force, perhaps using private military companies such as those that already protect humanitarian aid workers. This might be combined with a principle requiring automatic action when prespecified trigger points are reached. The African Union's constitution already mandates that a nondemocratic replacement of government of any of its member states results in automatic membership suspension, and this mandate has been applied repeatedly.[30]

The twelve design principles cannot guarantee peace, but they can help prevent peace from failing. No order of priority has been proposed or yet found; the order may be case-specific. Several of the principles apply to macroeconomics in violence-afflicted states. A fiscal policy that rewards constructive participation in rebuilding society rather than withholding benefits changes the payoffs for society's members and also links to the common value formation principle. Long-term investment or aid creates external vested interests in successful peace outcomes (e.g., China in Africa). Separating the functions of policy setting, fiscal disbursement, and service delivery goes with the principle of subsidiarity (devolution of decision-making to the local level) and that of self-policing enforcement (through service customers' ability to complain to the disbursement agency, which can then select an alternative supplier). Peace negotiators and aides should recognize that not only is the mere presence of economic principles in peace treaties important but that they should obey a higher-order set of principles also based in economics. Under the same set of challenging conditions, some states succumb to violence while others do not, and some states experience relatively strong economic growth while others do not.[31] Much of the difference has to do with the quality of the decision-making and decision-implementing institutions, which, in turn, has to do with whether the design of these institutions coheres with the higher-order principles outlined here. The World Bank's 2011 *World Development Report* reports at length on institutional legitimacy (authentic authority), inclusive-enough coalitions (formation of common values), and the need for sustained external support (creating vested interests). Our list is more comprehensive and more systematic—but in either case it is clear that the needed research has only just begun.

Third-Party Intervention

Third-party intervention, whether it is diplomacy, military action, or foreign aid, is not straightforward:[32] The Afghan and Iraqi wars of the 2000s show that even well-intentioned intervention can make life worse for violence-afflicted populations. Diplomatic involvement in the peace process can be vital. In some cases military support is necessary just to bring the parties to the negotiating table and keep them there. In Sierra Leone the involvement of British armed forces was important in forcing rebel leaders to negotiate. As discussed, aid can also be important, as can aid conditionality—the threat, or promise, of changing payoffs.[33]

Third parties are never only benevolent, however. They have interests and will bring these to bear: Cuba intervened in Angola, the United States in Vietnam, Russia in Afghanistan, NATO in the Balkans and in Libya. They may support one side more than the other, push their own agenda in negotiations, and tie aid to their own interests. Forced negotiation can legitimize the ruling positions of those who may have started armed conflict in the first place and may marginalize civil society, violating the principle of authentic authority.[34]

The quantitative academic literature on third-party intervention—theoretical and empirical—is only beginning to flourish. A useful distinction is between unilateral third-party intervention and multilateral third-party intervention, as multilateral intervention requires solving its own collective action problem, particularly that of free riding on others' contribution to solve a common problem. The likelihood is that only minimum levels of intervention will be agreed, perhaps too little to assist the parties and populations in conflict. In contrast, unilateral intervention requires no collective decision-making.[35] What, then, are its determinants? One author suggests eight relevant factors.[36] First, there must be information that something is amiss. Without it, nonconflict neighbors cannot do anything at all, and any humanitarian instinct that might exist cannot be activated. But even with information, nothing might be done on account of incapacity or apathy. Second is spillover—or noise—to nonconflict neighbors, such as refugees moving from one state to another. The more spillover, the more one might expect neighbors to intervene. Third is distance: The closer the neighbors, the more informed and caring they are. Fourth is relations, which can overcome distance. Colonial ties or immigrant groups with national origins in violence-afflicted states can make the former colonial power or the immigrant-host country more receptive to providing aid. Fifth is the din from neighbors: The more one is distracted from any one of them, the less one is inclined or able to offer assistance. Sixth is noise at home, which could prevent a state from aiding a neighbor: The more domestic problems a state has, the less it is willing or able to come to a neighbor's rescue. Seventh is economic and strategic self-interest, such as protecting trade routes or obtaining international stature (e.g., being seen as engaging in peacekeeping actions). Eighth is the opportunity for military (peacekeeping) training in real-time conditions.

Humanitarian goodwill is not among the determining factors; neither is budgetary cost. Peacekeeping tends to be done for rather more hard-edged reasons. Canada first burst onto the peacekeeping scene in 1956 to help a splintering NATO alliance that had been undermined when Washington told Paris and London to get out of the Suez region. Likewise, in 1960, when Belgium threatened to pull out of NATO over the unrest in Congo, Canada sent peacekeepers to that troubled African region. The peacekeeping in Cyprus, to which Canada contributed, was related to keeping NATO members Greece and Turkey at bay.[37] As to the budgetary cost of peacekeeping, despite protestations to the contrary, it is generally trivial—at least in relation to the cost of maintaining standing, national armies.

The list of factors can serve as a rapid assessment checklist to evaluate the likelihood that a third-party state will intervene to help create and guarantee the stability of peace and gauge the sincerity, and therefore desirability, of accepting or not accepting offers of help.

Institutions and Policies

In chapter 2, we suggested that any community consists of three societies: commercial, civil, and political. Commercial society allocates resources through markets, civil society allocates resources through moral suasion, and political society allocates resources through power. These societies should be well balanced. This applies to peacemaking and peacekeeping as well. The peacekeeping-related apparatus of political society includes institutions such as the United Nations, the Organization for Security and Cooperation in Europe (OSCE), the North Atlantic Treaty Organization (NATO), ASEAN, the Economic Community of West African States (ECOWAS), the Southern African Development Community (SADC), and other institutions as well. The AU and the European Union likewise are animals of political society: All are agreements among equal sovereigns.

The policies of the supranational institutions are constrained by a charter or founding articles that members agree to. The primary purpose of the United Nations as an international body is to prevent war from arising between states, but the organization is constrained by the veto powers of the five permanent members of its fifteen-member Security Council. This makes intervening in internal armed conflicts even more difficult, as it imposes on states' sovereignty. Action from the United Nations is mostly postwar. There are no standing peacekeeping forces, and each mission is debated on a case-by-case basis and, if approved, is time-limited. Forces and funds for each mission need to be found separately. The UN program budget for the two-year budget cycle 2010–11 was USD5.16 billion, or about USD2.6 billion per year. Other, separately funded UN activities add about another USD15 billion per year—and peacekeeping about USD7.3 billion in fiscal year 2010–11—so that the entirety of the UN annual budget is around USD20 billion. This is roughly equal to the budget of the New York City public school system, which was USD22 billion in fiscal year 2009–10.

Headquartered in Vienna, the OSCE is a regional security organization under Article VIII of the UN Charter, with fifty-six member states as of June 2011. It works on early warning, conflict prevention, crisis management, and postconflict rehabilitation. It is organized at the head-of-state level, convenes for occasional summits, and hosts an annual meeting of foreign ministers. With a budget of about EUR150 million, it employs nearly three thousand staff members and has seventeen field operations, mostly in Southeast and Central Europe and Central Asia. A weekly forum for security cooperation is held in Vienna, Austria, for issues pertaining to arms control and confidence- and security-building measures.

Both SADC and ECOWAS have fifteen members. Ostensibly economic development organizations organized at the political level—in contrast to the African Development Bank, which is a regional development finance body—they also both have peace- and security-related functions and organs. SADC, formed in 1980 and headquartered in Gaborone, Botswana, has an organ on politics, defense, and security cooperation, with a strategic plan that includes the political, defense, state security, and public security sectors. It also includes a regional peacekeeping training center located (perhaps ironically at present) in Zimbabwe. ECOWAS, formed in 1975, has a peace and security function as well and is institutionally run through a commission, a community parliament, a court of justice, and an investment and development bank. It contains a peace exchange forum, an (early) warning and response network, a small arms control program, and a standby force. It has issued an election monitoring declaration.

Headquartered in Jakarta, Indonesia, ASEAN now has ten members and sees itself as a political security, economic, and cultural development organization. Formed by five members in 1967 in Bangkok, Thailand, it has recently been reorganized and is based on a charter that entered into force on December 15, 2008. The charter provides legal status and an institutional framework for ASEAN and its work. An ASEAN Political-Security Community (APSC) is planned for implementation by 2015; members "pledge to rely exclusively on peaceful processes in the settlement of intra-regional differences and regard their security as fundamentally linked to one another and bound by geographic location, common vision and objectives."[38] A related organization is the ASEAN Regional Forum, which includes non-ASEAN states. Established in 1993, its twofold purpose is "to foster constructive dialogue and consultation on political and security issues of common interest and concern; and to make significant contributions to efforts towards confidence-building and preventive diplomacy in the Asia-Pacific region."[39] ASEAN also holds ministerial-level meetings on defense and on transnational crime.

All the supranational organizations recognize that politics (peace and security), economics, and culture are related and linked. But as interstate organizations they usually do not and cannot do much about strife within member states. This limitation does not apply to civil society organizations such as the International Committee of the Red Cross (ICRC) and numerous other NGOs, such as International Alert, the International Business Leaders Forum, Global Witness, or Amnesty International, or even to individual negotiators such as Martti Ahtisaari, who was awarded the Nobel Peace Prize in 2008. The ICRC, however, has struggled to shift its orientation as warfare has changed. Founded by a businessman in the 1850s, it was astonishingly successful at convening states to agree to what became the Geneva Conventions. These laid down rules to guide behavior in interstate war, particularly regarding the treatment of the wounded and of prisoners of war. But as security threats and wars have shifted toward civil war, terrorism, and drug and human trafficking, the Geneva Conventions have not applied. Into the breach sprang groups such as Médecins Sans Frontières (MSF). Its humanitarian emergency assistance functions are far removed from economics, but economic matters make their existence necessary. In the 1990s Global Witness singlehandedly created the topic of conflict diamonds, even as it has now withdrawn from the organization it helped create.[40]

Global Witness's work points to the principles of information, monitoring, and accountability and, in lesser degree, to that of self-policing enforcement. The ICRC today, meanwhile, functions mainly in terms of the information, monitoring, and accountability principles, although, like Global Witness, it is a form of media-driven accountability in the court of world opinion, a moral accountability. At present, only sovereign states can provide for accountability with consequential bite for war criminals, as in the authority given to the International Criminal Court. The political society organizations also are able, far more readily than others, to address the principles of changing payoffs, of creating vested interests and leadership, of graduated reciprocity and clarity, and of fostering and engaging in repeated, small steps in negotiation. But often they do so only after civil society organizations have brought attention to a need or misdeed in the first place. In short, the principles form a package: All are important, and the more these principles are explicitly recognized in the negotiation and design of peace agreements, the higher the likely probability of stable peace— and vice versa.

For commercial society, the stakes and incentives are very different. Businesses like revenue and dislike cost, and unfortunately for them, complying with rules and regulations across some two hundred state entities and tens of thousands of political entities at subnational and supranational levels is very costly. So are interstate war, civil war, and crime, as suppliers, employees, customers, and markets suffer. Increasingly, global companies recognize that their self-interest lies in fostering peace, not war. The absence of peace is not a useful business proposition: No markets, no money, no profit.

As business and economic globalization continue to be driven by reduced transport and communications costs, it is likely that business leaders will be increasingly interested in peace and security, if only to protect and grow markets. Peace negotiators should not overlook the constructive role of consulting with business leaders whose companies operate in postwar areas or violence-riven zones. The International Organization for Standardization (ISO) is increasingly involved in standard setting outside of the narrow technical product specification arena in which it started (e.g., ISO film speed standards); ISO9000 sets quality management standards and ISO14000 sets environmental management standards. Security standards for biometrics, cybersecurity, and "societal security" in cases of industrial accidents, along with similar security issues pertaining to company operations, are in active discussion. While these are mainly related to risk management, and at least in part designed to limit exposure to legal liability that might arise from industrial accidents, it is not inconceivable that, some years into the future, a family of standards may emerge on company behavior regarding complicity in human rights violations, relations to security forces, and the like that, for now, are restricted to the realms of political and civil society.

Standardization lowers costs, improves product and service quality, and thus attracts customers that provide revenue. As local, national, and global companies are hurt by violence, ISO may well develop an ISO security standard—say, ISO50000—that specifies how companies engage in and deal with public policy issues such as peace and security. In terms of our principles, that of creating vested (commercial) interests beyond the state would apply, as would that of common value formation (among global business leaders, who are becoming ever more divorced from the quaintness of nationality and national identity) and that of creating conflict resolution mechanisms. The International Chamber of Commerce—not a chamber of chambers, but an organization of global corporations—has its own conflict mediation, arbitration, and court system, the rulings of which many state judicial systems accept as binding. Thus, the global commercial sector sometimes can and does transcend state boundaries as if it were itself a sovereign, rule-setting, and rule-enforcing player. On World Standards Day in 2000, the leaders of three world standards organizations—the ISO, the

FIGURE 5.1. Nepal, 1960–2009

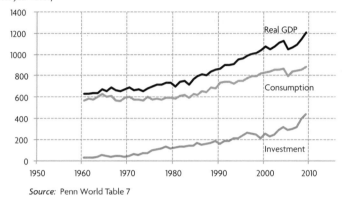

Inflation, population, and purchasing power parity–adjusted per capita GDP, consumption, and investment (I$, base year = 2005)

Source: Penn World Table 7

International Electrotechnical Commission (IEC), and the International Telecommunication Union (ITU)—stated that

> without agreement, there can be no peace. And without peace, there can be no lasting prosperity. International standards are an essential tool in mankind's continuing efforts to achieve more of both.[41]

That the commercial sector has largely been left out of considerations in peace negotiations is a mistake. Fortunately, it can easily be rectified.

FAILURE AND SUCCESS: Two Case Studies

FAILURE: NEPAL

Nepal's convoluted post–World War II history is entangled with China's incorporation of Tibet and India's consequent counteraction by seeking influence in and through Nepal. King Mahendra (r. 1955–72) abandoned an incipient experiment with multiparty democracy in 1959. The data series in figure 5.1 starts in 1960. King Bihendra (r. 1972–2001) was compelled in 1989 to agree to constitutional changes that led to the seating of a multiparty parliament in 1991. In 1996 a Maoist insurgency movement began a ten-year period of armed violence, attempting to replace the royal parliamentary system with a socialist republic. The figure shows that investment stalled during this period. Following Bihendra's murder, due to an intrafamily squabble, King Gyanendra inherited the throne (r. 2001–06). In 2005 he dismissed government and parliament, took executive power, and declared rule under martial law. Consumption, investment, and GDP fell. By this time a stalemate had developed between Maoist forces and government troops. Also, the king's moves inspired broad opposition. Parliamentary leaders fled to India, formed a seven-party alliance (SPA), and signed a twelve-point understanding with the Maoist party. They all agreed to unseat the king and form a democracy with contested elections in which all could compete for votes. Reinstated in 2006, parliament voted to abolish the monarchy. This obtained in May 2008, after an election the prior month resulted in the Maoists obtaining the largest number of seats in a constituent assembly. Under Maoist leadership, the assembly voted to end monarchy and declare the country a federal republic. The Maoists formed the new government. This new government, however, was toppled in May 2009 and a Marxist-Leninist party took power. The initial postmonarchy political transition and peace negotiations were insufficiently inclusive and left various interests disaffected enough to restart violence. At a minimum, the Nepali peace efforts violated the principles of authentic authority and common value formation. Unrest continues as of June 2011.

Economically, the country's real per capita growth rate in measured economic output was a mere 0.75 percent between 1961 and 1969, 0.95 percent in the 1970s, and 1.59 percent, 1.92 percent, and 1.64 percent in the 1980s, 1990s, and 2000s, respectively. The economy is propped up in large part by hundreds of thousands of Nepalis working abroad and remitting funds back home and also by Nepal's foreign exchange earnings for UN peacekeeping services rendered. From 1988 to 2000 the share of military expenditure in GDP was one percentage point or less and since then has at times climbed to over two percentage points, so that Nepal's civilian GDP growth rate is smaller than the 1.64 percent of the 2000s suggests. Even at that rate, however, the Nepalese economy would need about forty-three years to double in size to about I$2,400 per capita—just over half the I$4,600 its more peaceable neighbor Bhutan achieved in 2009.

Nepal still is waiting for a reconstructed social contract, one inclusive enough, as the World Bank would call it, to reflect genuine authentic authority vested in government so that it can commence with the business of governing. There were and are plenty of vested outside interests at play, such as those of India and China, but they are not pulling in the same direction and are also entwined with subcontinental power plays (among Burma,

FIGURE 5.2. South Africa, 1950–2009

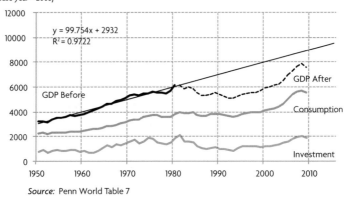

Source: Penn World Table 7

Kashmir-Pakistan, Afghanistan) and internal problems (Tibet, northeast India). Finally, as Nepal is a small economy wedged in between two giants, the commercial society appears not to have been engaged. Money is to be made elsewhere, and so Nepalese businesses do not have much at stake, especially considering the risk of possibly offending Nepal's larger neighbors.

SUCCESS: SOUTH AFRICA

South Africa's regime of racial segregation and discrimination collapsed with the end of the Cold War. By April 1994 a wholesale political change— mostly peaceful—had taken place in the country. The African National Congress (ANC) won elections in April of that year and Nelson Mandela became the country's president.

As figure 5.2 shows, from 1950 to 1980 South Africa experienced steady, linear economic growth. Undoubtedly, growth would have been faster if the country's nonwhite population had not been suppressed and excluded from accumulating human capital and contributing more productively to the economy. From year to year, growth was also more uneven than the overall trend might suggest: about 1.8 percent per capita per year in the 1950s, 3.2 percent in the 1960s, and 1.1 percent in the 1970s. Following the Soweto uprising and 1976 and, in 1977, the murder of Steve Biko, a student and antiapartheid activist, black South African labor unions became more restive and the international political community placed economic sanctions on South Africa. By 1980 GDP growth had stalled. Investment per person during the decade of the 1980s fell drastically and per capita consumption flattened out. For the remainder of the apartheid years, inflation-adjusted per capita GDP experienced an average annual decline of 1.4 percent from 1981 to 1993 (inclusive), mostly driven by declining investment. Per capita GDP in 1993 was about what it had been in 1969—as if there had been nearly a quarter century without economic progress.

The domestic business community played an important but poorly recognized and underreported role in the political transition. According to International Alert, in 1985 a delegation of business and media representatives met with ANC leaders in Zambia. This meeting and others had a dual effect. White business acknowledged the ANC's political legitimacy long before white politics did, and it also introduced the ANC—which had embraced a socialist economy ideology—to capitalist, free market economics. A bargain was struck that both parties adhered to: Businesses pushed for political change, and in time, the ANC reciprocated with economic policies that aimed at improving the lot of the poor, but nonetheless recognized that private business interests can generate employment, income, and tax revenue. Figure 5.2 shows that following the 1994 transition, the country moved back to the trend in growth it left in 1980. From 1994 to 2009 growth averaged nearly 2.6 percent per person per year. However, the figure also reveals that investment levels did not increase for about ten years after apartheid and only in 2009 began to reach levels seen thirty years before.

The country is a success in managing the political transition peacefully, though it may yet fail due to extraordinarily high unemployment rates and crime levels, abysmal failures in its primary and secondary education system, and its continuing HIV/AIDS health crisis. A relentless focus on asset building to spur economic growth will be required to secure political stability in years to come. It appears that a sense of a broad cross-racial social contract exists, even as individuals engage in criminal behavior. The difficulty lies not with the social contract but with its enforcement. Multilateral third-party intervention, driven by the moral outrage of global civil society and agreed to by global business and policymakers, helped bring apartheid down, though not until the collapse of the Soviet Union undermined the last illusory vestiges of self-justification and anticommunist rhetoric within the Boer white community that had held the reins of power. Today, most South Africans appear to share common values and pride in their country, despite difficulties in their daily lives, and democracy—authentic authority—if not free of problems, is deemed to work.

Policy Lessons and Tips

LESSON 5.1: A well-functioning social contract lies at the heart of internally and externally peaceful societies. Societies have to agree on norms, standards, and rules of social behavior.

LESSON 5.2: There are no principles of peace that guarantee success. But there are principles that, if not followed, might spell failure. They are the principle of changing payoffs, creating vested interests and leadership, graduated reciprocity and clarity, engaging in repeated small steps, common value formation, authentic authority, subsidiarity, conflict resolution mechanisms, information and monitoring, of accountability, self-policing enforcement, and nesting.

LESSON 5.3: Multilateral third-party intervention is plagued by free-riding behavior. Likely factors determining the net benefit of unilateral third-party intervention include information, noise, distance, relations, din, noise at home, self-interest, and opportunity. This rapid assessment list can help to gauge the sincerity and desirability of accepting or not accepting offers of help.

LESSON 5.4: Political, civil, and commercial society all need to be engaged in peacemaking and peacekeeping. To restrict economic and other aspects of peace treaty negotiations and postwar reconstruction to political players alone without consulting with civil and commercial society addresses only the short-term immediacy of silencing guns rather than the long-term necessity of rebuilding social foundations for civic and commercial reengagement. It risks undermining the social contract.

Notes

1. UNDP, *Post-Conflict Economic Recovery*, 17.
2. In the 2000s, 90 percent of all thirty-nine violent conflicts that started during the decade also had conflict in previous decades. See World Bank, *World Development Report 2011*, 58, Table 1.2.

3. UNDP, *Post-Conflict Economic Recovery,* 17.

4. UNDP, *Post-Conflict Economic Recovery,* 20.

5. Recent Nobel Prize awards in economics have recognized this, e.g., to Schelling in 2005, Hurwicz, Maskin, and Myerson in 2007, and Ostrom and Williamson in 2009.

6. D. McFadden, "Free Markets and Fettered Consumers," presidential address, American Economic Association, Boston, MA, January 7, 2006, available at http://elsa.berkeley.edu/~mcfadden/ (accessed December 6, 2011).

7. R.H. Thaler and C.R. Sunstein, *Nudge: Improving Decisions about Health, Wealth, and Happiness* (New Haven, CT: Yale University Press, 2008).

8. See, e.g., K. Binmore, *Natural Justice* (New York: Oxford University Press, 2005), on the evolution of fairness norms, moral codes, and notions of justice.

9. There is no presumption that a unique and uniform structure exists; more likely, multiple structures can result in satisfactory outcomes.

10. Some scholars have noted that social capital can be counterproductive. If it consists of trust and network strength, then criminal networks work better when they have more social capital. See also P. Seabright, *The Company of Strangers: A Natural History of Economic Life* (Princeton, NJ: Princeton University Press, 2004).

11. See http://www.unfetteredmind.org/money-meditation; see also J. Brauer, "Money and Values," *Stone Garden Economics,* available at http://stonegardeneconomics.com/blog/?p=993 (accessed January 13, 2012).

12. Mansoob Murshed, "Conflict as the Absence of Contract," *The Economics of Peace and Security Journal,* vol. 4, no. 1 (2009), 35.

13. Murshed "Conflict as the Absence of Contract," 36.

14. See D. Fischer, *Nonmilitary Aspects of Security: A Systems Approach* (Aldershot, UK: Dartmouth, 1993).

15. This section is based on J. Brauer and D. Fischer, "Building Institutions for Peacemaking and Peacekeeping," in J. Brauer, J. Galbraith, and L. Webster, eds., *Economics of Peace and Security* (Oxford: EOLSS, 2009), 148–159; J. Brauer, "Developing Peacemaking Institutions: An Economist's Approach," in Geoff Harris, ed., *Achieving Security in Sub-Saharan Africa: Cost-Effective Alternatives to the Military* (Pretoria, South Africa: Institute for Security Studies, 2004), 137–153; J. Brauer, "Theory and Practice of Intervention," *The Economics of Peace and Security Journal,* vol. 1, no. 2 (2006), 17–23. This work is grounded in R. Axelrod, *The Evolution of Cooperation* (New York: Basic Books, 1984); E. Ostrom, *Governing the Commons: The Evolution of Institutions for Collective Action* (Cambridge: Cambridge University Press, 1990); T. Sandler, *Global Challenges: An Approach to Environmental, Political, and Economic Problems* (Cambridge: Cambridge University Press, 1997); and others.

16. J. Brauer and R. Caruso, "Economists and Peacebuilding," in R. MacGintry, ed., *Handbook of Peacebuilding* (London: Routledge, forthcoming).

17. "With the relative lack of easily extractable natural assets in Mozambique (compared to say Angola or Liberia) the end of war was endogenously determined.

Neither the government nor RENAMO were able to sustain the fighting finan-
cially and the drought of 1991–93 finally forced a settlement." T. Brück, "War and
Reconstruction in Northern Mozambique," *The Economics of Peace and Security
Journal,* vol. 1, no. 1 (2006), 31. Running out of money is not just a modern-day
reason to end war. See, e.g., C. Marichal, *Bankruptcy of Empire: Mexican Silver and
the Wars between Spain, Britain, and France, 1760–1810* (New York: Cambridge
University Press, 2007), on the difficulty of the Spanish empire to continue war
with France and England when its Mexican colony became independent and the
flow of bullion stopped. Similarly, Austria, Prussia, and Russia in squabbles during
the reign of Frederick the Great (1740–86) needed at least periodic breaks from
war whenever the tills were exhausted; see U. Oster, *Preußen: Geschichte eines
Königreichs* (München: Piper Verlag, 2011). The invention of war bonds was, not
least, related to the need to finance war; see Ferguson, *Ascent of Money.*

18. A real-world example: "In October 1996, one year after the Dayton peace negotia-
    tions, Carl Bildt, the international community's high representative in Bosnia,
    faced a crisis. Momcilo Krajisnik, a close associate of indicted war criminal Rado-
    van Karadzic, had just been elected to Bosnia's three-person collective presiden-
    cy, but in a gesture of continuing Bosnian Serb defiance toward Dayton's goal of a
    united Bosnia, he now refused to attend the presidential swearing-in ceremony in
    Sarajevo. His refusal threatened to undermine the fragile new Bosnian state from
    its inception. Bildt responded by dispatching his senior deputy for economic re-
    construction to the Bosnian Serb headquarters in Pale, accompanied by the resi-
    dent representatives of the World Bank, the European Bank for Reconstruction
    and Development, and the European Union, and President Clinton's special envoy
    for reconstruction. Together they delivered a stern warning: Not one penny of
    reconstruction aid would flow to the Serb Republic if Krajisnik failed to appear.
    Four days later, Krajisnik was in Sarajevo for the ceremony." Quoted from J. Boyce
    and M. Pastor, Jr., "Aid for Peace: Can International Financial Institutions Help
    Prevent Conflict?," *World Policy Journal,* vol. 15, no. 2 (1998), 42.

19. Only very recently has the literature formally recognized that third-party inter-
    vention need not be with the intention of creating peace. See Yang-Ming Chang,
    Shane Sanders, and Bhavneet Walia, "Conflict Persistence and the Role of Third-
    Party Interventions," *The Economics of Peace and Security Journal,* vol. 5, no. 1
    (2010), 30–33; Joel Potter and John L. Scott, "Issues in Third-Party Intervention
    Research and the Role of Destruction in Conflict," *The Economics of Peace and
    Security Journal,* vol. 5, no. 1 (2010), 26–29. See also below.

20. Intervention can also be of an unwitting kind: China's economic ascendance has
    stimulated its greater participation in world raw materials markets. If only for the
    security of its own investments, it has been drawn into Africa's squabbles and will
    need to make at least a marginal contribution to peace and security to safeguard
    its resource extraction and supply lines.

21. T. Schelling, *Micromotives and Macrobehavior* (New York: Norton, 1978).

22. Schelling, *Micromotives.* He backs this up mathematically. Also see A. Sen, *Iden-
    tity and Violence: The Illusion of Destiny* (New York: Norton, 2006); G.A. Akerlof

and R.E. Kranton, "Economics and Identity," *Quarterly Journal of Economics,* vol. 155, no. 3 (2000), 715–753; and G.A. Akerlof and R.E. Kranton, *Identity Economics: How Our Identities Shape Our Work, Wages, and Well-Being* (Princeton, NJ: Princeton University Press, 2010), on economics of identity.

23. Transcendence can be abused, of course, as in the common value formation to arouse one group against another on the pretext of religious or other beliefs.

24. Representation requires recognition that those who become part of the negotiation team are chosen by a process that itself is a collective action. One cannot simply assume that party A and party B are unitary actors. Instead, one must often assume that within-party interests play out as well, which may make it impossible for the official party A and party B negotiators to actually negotiate anything at all. See, e.g., Anderton and Carter, *Principles of Conflict Economics,* and literature cited therein.

25. A.O. Hirschman, *Exit, Voice, and Loyalty: Responses to Decline in Firms, Organizations, and States* (Cambridge, MA: Harvard University Press, 1970); Ostrom, *Governing the Commons.*

26. Sandler, *Global Challenges,* 38–40.

27. Global Commission on Drug Policy, *War on Drugs: Report of the Global Commission on Drug Policy,* 2011, available at www.globalcommissionondrugs.org (accessed December 6, 2011).

28. Global Commission on Drug Policy, *War on Drugs.*

29. Axelrod, *Evolution of Cooperation.*

30. The idea of automaticity was proposed in J. Brauer, "Regional Peace as an International Public Good: Collective Action in Southern Africa," in J. Brauer and K. Hartley, eds., *The Economics of Regional Security: NATO, the Mediterranean, and Southern Africa* (Amsterdam: Harwood Academic Publishers, 2000), 313–314. On the economics of private military companies, see J. Brauer, and H. van Tuyll, *Castles, Battles, and Bombs: How Economics Explains Military History* (Chicago: University of Chicago Press, 2008), chapter 8; see also D. Richemond-Barak, "Rethinking Private Warfare," *Law and Ethics of Human Rights,* vol. 5, no. 1 (2011), article 5, available at http://www.bepress.com/lehr/vol5/iss1/art5 (accessed December 6, 2011).

31. See Murshed, "Conflict as the Absence of Contract"; UNDP, *Post-Conflict Economic Recovery.*

32. This section is based on Brauer, "Theory and Practice of Intervention," esp. 19–20.

33. J. Boyce, "Aid, Conditionality, and War Economies," working paper no. 70, Political Economy Research Institute, Amherst, MA, 2003.

34. M. Kaldor, *New and Old Wars,* 2nd ed. (Cambridge: Polity, 2006).

35. That is, other than within the state of the unilateral intervener. But in the case of the United States and most other sovereign states, decision-making is effectively delegated to the head of state. Thus, George W. Bush, by avoiding calling the results of his decisions wars, could send armed forces to Afghanistan and Iraq with-

out a formal vote in the U.S. Congress that the U.S. Constitution otherwise would have required.

36. Brauer, "Theory and Practice of Intervention."

37. Historian D. Morton comments: "Peacekeeping might be idealistic, but it also fitted Cold War needs." See *Understanding Canadian Defence* (Toronto: Penguin Canada and McGill Institute, 2003), 17.

38. Quoted from ASEAN, "ASEAN Political-Security Community," available at http://www.aseansec.org/18741.htm (accessed December 6, 2011).

39. Quoted from http://aseanregionalforum.asean.org/about.html (accessed January 13, 2012). As of June 2011, the members were Australia, Bangladesh, Brunei Darussalam, Cambodia, Canada, China, Democratic People's Republic of Korea, European Union, India, Indonesia, Japan, Laos, Malaysia, Myanmar, Mongolia, New Zealand, Pakistan, Papua New Guinea, Philippines, Republic of Korea, the Russian Federation, Singapore, Sri Lanka, Thailand, Timor-Leste, the United States, and Vietnam.

40. Global Witness, "Global Witness Leaves Kimberley Process, Calls for Diamond Trade to Be Held Accountable," December 5, 2011, available at http://www.global-witness.org/library/global-witness-leaves-kimberley-process-calls-diamond-trade-be-held-accountable (accessed January 29, 2012).

41. See International Organization for Standardization, "International Standards for Peace and Prosperity 31st World Standards Day 14 October 2000," available at http://www.iso.org/iso/pressrelease.htm?refid=Ref780 (accessed December 6, 2011).

APPENDIX A
Classifications of Violence and Armed Actors

In addition to the WHO's ecology of violence,[1] the Geneva Declaration on Armed Violence and Development (GD) notes that violence comes in many forms. Violence against women includes intimate partner violence, sexual violence, honor killing, dowry-related violence, acid attacks, female infanticide, and sex-selective abortions.[2] Organized crime, armed gang violence as well as extrajudicial killings, and disappearances are forms of violence associated with criminal activity and the miscarriage of justice by officers of law and order institutions. Politically motivated violence includes mob violence, lynchings, rebellions, insurrections, and civil war.

Another typology lists the following forms of violence, with violence indicators in parentheses:[3]

- Political violence (assassinations, bomb attacks, kidnappings, torture, genocide, mass displacements, riots);

- Routine state violence (violent law enforcement activities, encounter killings, social cleansing operations, routine torture);

- Economic and crime-related violence (armed robbery, extortions, kidnappings for ransom, control of markets through violence);

- Community and informal justice and policing (lynching, vigilante action, mob justice); and

- Postwar displacements and disputes (clashes over land, revenge killings, small-scale ethnic cleansing).

A typology of armed actors rather than of the violence they may engage in is available in a paper by Muggah and Jütersonke.[4] It overlays types of armed actors on a vertical grid of organized versus spontaneous violence with a horizontal grid of state versus nonstate actors.

Notes

1. World Health Organization (WHO), *World Report on Violence and Health,* ed. E.G. Krug, L.L. Dahlberg, J.A. Mercy, A.B. Zwi, and R. Lozano (Geneva: WHO, 2002).

ment, *Global Burden of Armed Violence* (Geneva: Geneva Declaration Secretariat, 2009).

3. Torunn Chaudhary and Astri Suhrke, "Postwar Violence," unpublished background paper, Small Arms Survey, Geneva, 2008, as cited in Geneva Declaration, *Global Burden,* 65.

4. Robert Muggah and Oliver Jütersonke, "Endemic Urban Violence and Public Security," in *Cities and Urban Violence* (Ottawa: Ministry of Foreign Affairs, 2008).

APPENDIX B
General Characteristics of Case Countries

The ten illustrative cases in this text are structured such that we cover both historical and contemporary cases; war, civil war (grievance- and greed-based), and postwar criminalization of an economy; and all geographic regions: Europe, Africa, the Americas, Asia, and Asia-Pacific. Of course, not every failure is a failure in every respect, and not every success is a success in every respect. Many countries can be placed in either category, depending on what aspect one wishes to emphasize. Timor-Leste suffered massive violent upheavals in the late 1990s and early 2000s. Political independence came in 2002 and violence recurred in 2006. After protracted negotiations, the country now enjoys high revenue flows from offshore oil and gas deposits but suffers from utterly inadequate infrastructure, especially roads to connect markets, and very high poverty rates.

We hope that in the future a large set of case studies will be based on the chapters' lessons and the principles of peacemaking and peacekeeping that we identified. This would help to test our views, at least in a qualitative sense, until quantitative measures can be developed to apply formal statistical tests. The more we learn about the structure of peace and peacemaking, the better.

APPENDIX C
Glossary

aggregate demand: the summation of demand by various categories of buyers. Usually written as the sum of consumption by private households; investment by firms; government spending at the federal, provincial, and district or municipal levels; and the difference between the values of exports and imports. The value of exports represents demand from overseas for domestically produced goods. The value of imports is subtracted because it reflects demand realized in another economy.

aggregate demand/aggregate supply framework (AD/AS model): a single visual representation that pulls together virtually all relevant demand- and supply-side variables, considers all actors (private and public), integrates domestic and foreign sectors, and simultaneously considers the short and the long term. Although economists do not agree on this framework as an explanatory device, they do agree on it as a heuristic device, the point of departure for agreement and disagreement, of refinements and extensions, and the model in contrast to which alternative representations of economies are constructed. It is also the point of departure for policy debates and recommendations.

asset stripping: the depletion of the stock of capital to serve current consumption needs, thereby diminishing society's capacity to produce in the future.

assets: those that make production possible. Assets include natural, physical, human, social, or institutional capital. Assets are needed to produce goods and services.

balance of payments (BoP): an accounting framework that tracks the monetary value of a country's imports and exports of goods and services as well as the corresponding financial flows; the framework consists of credits (inflows) and debits (outflows), which, by definition, must sum to zero.

bathtub theorem: a concept used to understand the idea of building a stock of assets. If the inflow of water into a bathtub represents production and the outflow represents consumption, then an excess of the flow of production over the flow of consumption adds to the stock of available goods; conversely, an excess of consumption over production diminishes the stock.

capital: an input into production. Capital includes physical capital, such as machinery, equipment, and physical structures or facilities that one may have available to work with; the natural capital of the planet Earth, that is, raw materials that can go into production processes (some renewable, others not); human capital, including peoples' talents, ingenuity, skills, training, education, knowledge, and experience; and social capital, an economic asset consisting of the social and communal networks humans build.

choice architecture: the self-conscious and deliberate design of incentives that inhibit undesired and promote desired individual behavior, such that a social system as a whole moves toward a desired outcome.

classical growth theory: a theory of economic growth arguing that any production surplus for the current population will, in time, be consumed by population growth, so that societies will repetitively revert to subsistence levels of existence. Thus sustained economic growth per capita is impossible.

collective violence: a category of violence that includes armed conflict between, among, and within states, communal-level violence, violent acts of terror, and organized crime.

creative destruction: coined by Joseph Schumpeter, a term referring to the idea that, in pursuit of profit opportunities, entrepreneurs in a competitive economy bring to market innovative products and processes that, on the one hand, destroy competing lines of business, but on the other hand are so revolutionary as to move the entire economic system forward.

currency appreciation/depreciation: the process by which one unit of home currency can buy a larger/smaller amount of foreign currency than before; under appreciation/depreciation, the home currency is said to have become stronger/weaker. An appreciating currency eases imports but hinders exports as foreign products become relatively cheaper to home customers and home products relative more expensive to foreign customers. A depreciating currency has the opposite effect.

currency defense: the attempt by monetary authorities to maintain the foreign exchange value of the home currency.

current account: part of a country's balance of payments, it reflects the monetary value of a country's international trade in goods and services.

current cost of violence: the direct and indirect cost of violence in a given time period within a given geographical space.

dynamic peace dividend: results when security, relief, and other war-related spending can be cut and applied to productivity-enhancing physical, human, institutional, and social capital.

economic growth: the percentage increase in economic output from one year to the next; it does not inform about income distribution or other aspects of well-being.

economic growth policy: policy that focuses primarily on asset growth and asset productivity growth and long-term opportunities for production and income generation, and less on distribution and consumption; in contrast to economic development policy, it assumes more of a constitutional and quantitative character.

economic development policy: policy that is somewhat more concerned with qualitative and equity aspects, such as rural development, the well-being of women, youth, and the elderly, and minority or disadvantaged population segments; some also include measures of personal happiness and community vitality and resilience.

economics: a field of study dealing with the production, distribution, and consumption of the means to livelihood, with the aim of continual betterment of life.

enabling policy conditions: the conditions for stable economic growth. These include well-functioning, transparent policymaking and policy implementing institutions, well-trained and accountable officials, and a predictable regulatory framework.

endogenous: arising from within an economic system and thus amenable to change by policy.

exogenous: affecting an economic system from outside the system and thus beyond policymakers' influence.

financial and capital account: an account that records nontrade flows in the balance of payments.

fiscal policy: policy concerned with how public sector revenue is raised and how that revenue is spent. It is not a crisis management tool; its primary function is to promote society's orderly development and well-being, that is, its economic growth and continual betterment. In crisis, spending fiscal resources on macroeconomic stabilization can be a necessary but costly distraction from its primary purpose.

flexible exchange rate regime: regime under which a country's monetary authorities normally will not intervene in the private markets that determine the value of the country's currency.

government net worth: government assets (e.g., formal ownership of infrastructure such as public highways, seaports, airports, and marine and land resources) minus government liabilities (e.g., pension liabilities, public debt obligations).

gross domestic product (GDP): the monetary value (and hence income) of all goods and services legally produced by residents of a country within one calendar year.

gross world product (GWP): the sum of gross domestic product across all countries.

horizontal tax equity: a situation in which persons who are equal in every respect are treated equally in taxation as well.

inflation: the change in average prices of goods and services produced, or consumed, from one time period to the next.

institutional and evolutionary economics: the study of economies as social systems. Among the institutions under scrutiny, which may be formal or informally constituted, are free trade, a minimal regulatory system, sound money, good law and order, secure property rights, corruption-free government, and a panoply of other good governance factors that together provide economic framework conditions.

international dollars (I\$): an artificial currency created to make the purchasing power of different currencies comparable across countries.

international financial institutions (IFIs): referring in the main to the International Monetary Fund (IMF) and the World Bank Group (WBG) at the global level, but also to regional development banks, such as the African Development Bank (AfDB), the Asian Development Bank (ADB), the Inter-American Development Bank (IADB), and the European Bank for Reconstruction and Development (EBRD).

interpersonal violence: a category of violence that includes intimate partner and other family violence, assault and homicide, and violence committed in institutional settings.

leader: an external actor able to organize changes in the payoff structure and/or the rules of the game in negotiations.

legacy cost of violence: the cost of past violence that carries over to the present.

long-run aggregate supply (LRAS): an economy's inherent productive capacity—its sheer potential to generate output—regardless of whether or not that capacity is productively employed or lies idle.

macroeconomic stabilization: attempt to moderate erratic swings in the business cycle through policy; tools include fiscal and monetary policy, even though macroeconomic stabilization is not their primary purpose and may in fact detract from that purpose.

monetary policy: policy dealing with the internal and external (foreign exchange) value of a state's currency, the determination of interest rates, and the regulation and supervision of the banking system.

money demand: demand for currency (cash and bank deposits).

money supply: the sum of cash and bank deposits (checking and saving) available for the purpose of conducting purchases now or in future (present consumption or, via saving, future consumption).

monitoring: collecting, processing, and verifying information, including the information and actions of another player.

national saving: private domestic saving plus government sector saving; this, plus foreign sector saving, finances private domestic investment.

natural resource rents: earnings from the sale of natural resources.

neoclassical growth theory: theory focusing on the causal relations between and among factors such as labor, savings, capital, investment, and technological change to predict output and output growth; under it, sustainable growth is deemed possible.

new classical growth theory: theory growing out of neoclassical growth theory that emphasizes understanding the institutional conditions needed to encourage entrepreneurship and make technological change and human capital formation possible.

nominal GDP: gross domestic product not adjusted for the effects of price inflation.

peace economics: the economic study and design of political, economic, and cultural institutions, their interrelations, and their policies to prevent, mitigate, or resolve any type of latent or actual violence or other destructive conflict within and between societies.

policy: a set of rules, directions, or guidelines to be followed for a particular issue area.

production possibilities frontier (PPF): the maximum possible production levels of a set of goods and services, given currently available levels of labor, capital, and other requisite production inputs.

purchasing power: the buying power of a unit of currency from one year to the next.

purchasing power parity: a statistical way to estimate the comparative purchasing power of different currency units, e.g., Indian rupees to New Zealand dollars, on the presumption that what matters is the service rendered, not the monetary unit used to pay for it; this permits comparisons across countries regardless of the value of their respective currencies' formal exchange rate values.

purchasing power parity dollars: see international dollars (I$).

quantity theory of money: a theory arguing that overly rapid increases in money supply eventually result in corresponding increases in inflation.

real GDP: gross domestic product adjusted for price inflation so that GDP values are comparable across years.

rent seeking: activities that generate unearned income by seeking to rewrite political, economic, and cultural rules in one's favor rather than earning income through fair competitive and productive effort.

rule of 70: a handy guide to compute the approximate number of years it takes for an economy to double in size.

self-harm: self-directed violence, including suicide.

short-run aggregate supply (SRAS): the supply of goods and services to the economy by the business sector in response to changes in the market price that can be obtained.

social contract: a framework of widely agreed-upon rules, social cohesion, and trust, along with external or self-policing enforcing institutions.

spillover cost of violence: costs of violence imposed on bystanders (e.g., refugees from state A that flee to and impose a cost on state B).

static peace dividend: a redistribution of economic activity from violence-related to nonviolence-related spending (e.g., from criminal to civil law for lawyers' activities).

statistical discrepancy: in the balance of payments, the difference between the current account and the financial and capital account.

sustainable developmental growth: a concept suggesting that growth without development is dangerous and development without growth infeasible; growth must serve developmental purposes and be ecologically sustainable.

velocity: the turnover rate of money; the frequency with which any specific unit of currency (dollar, euro, yen, etc.) is used in a given time period.

vertical tax equity: a situation in which those capable of paying more taxes are taxed at higher rates.

INDEX

Page numbers followed by *t*, *f*, and *n* indicate tables, figures, and footnotes, respectively.

ABOUT THE AUTHORS

Jurgen Brauer is professor of economics at the James M. Hull College of Business, Augusta State University, Augusta, GA. This primer was researched, written, and revised while he held visiting appointments in the economics departments of Chulalongkorn University, Bangkok, Thailand, Universidad del Rosario, Bogotá, Colombia, and the Institute of Economics, University of Barcelona, Spain.

J. Paul Dunne is professor of economics at the School of Economics, University of Cape Town, South Africa. His contribution to this primer was made during visiting professorships in the economics department of Chulalongkorn University, Bangkok, Thailand, the Faculty of Business Administration, Economics, and Political Science at the British University in Egypt, Cairo, and a professorship at the Bristol Business School, University of the West of England, Bristol, UK.

UNITED STATES INSTITUTE OF PEACE PRESS